Fodor's
25 Best

PARIS

Contents

KEY TO SYMBOLS

- 🚩 Map reference to the accompanying pull-out map
- ✉ Address
- ☎ Telephone number
- 🕐 Opening/closing times
- 🍽 Restaurant or café
- 🚉 Nearest rail station
- Ⓜ Nearest Métro (subway) station
- 🚌 Nearest bus route

ENTERTAINMENT 130

Whether you're after a cultural fix or just want a place to relax with a drink after a hard day's sight-seeing, we've made the best choices for you.

EAT 140

Uncover great dining experiences, from a quick bite at lunch to top-notch evening meals.

SLEEP 152

We've brought together the best hotels in the city, whatever budget you're on.

NEED TO KNOW 160

The practical information you need to make your trip run smoothly.

PULL-OUT MAP

The pull-out map accompanying this book is a comprehensive street plan of the city. We've given grid references within the book for each sight and listing.

⛴ Nearest riverboat or ferry stop	💷 Admission charges:
♿ Facilities for visitors with	Expensive (over €10),
disabilities	Moderate (€4–€10) and
ℹ Tourist information	Inexpensive (under €4)
❓ Other practical information	▷ Further information

Introducing Paris

The City of Light needs no introduction: the Eiffel Tower, Sacré-Cœur, the Louvre. It is not a museum, however, but a vibrant urban area. The monuments won't change, but everything else will. Forget stereotypes and see the city with new eyes.

Paris has been making a concerted effort to change its image as a cold city full of rude, arrogant people. That reputation was never entirely deserved, but the good news for both visitors and residents is that Paris has undergone many changes for the better. The mayor's office and the national government sponsor a number of popular (and free) annual events along the lines of the *Fête de la Musique* (21 June), which bring the normally reserved Parisians out to have fun.

In addition to *Paris Plage*, when the Right Bank of the Seine becomes a sandy beach for one month in the summer, the city is the site of *La Nuit des Musées* (May), when several museums stay open all night; *Les Journées du Patrimoine* (September), when normally off-limits monuments are open; *La Nuit Blanche* (October), with all-night art and cultural events; and outdoor music concerts in the summer.

And Paris is no longer deserted in August. Once transformed into a quiet village while the entire working population holidayed elsewhere, the city has come back to life as the French learn to stagger their holidays. It's still quiet, but more and more restaurants and shops are open. Picnicking in the city is now popular and the banks of the Seine and parks are full of outdoor diners. The once-forbidden lawns in its parks and squares are covered with children and sunbathers.

Most visitors come to see the great monuments, however. Having miraculously survived wars and revolution—some of them for a thousand years—they now seem to be eternal.

In recent years, much effort has gone into improving the quality of life in Paris, with projects like the Vélib' bicycle hire scheme (▷ 167) and *Paris Plage* enjoyed by Parisians and visitors alike.

FACTS AND FIGURES

Population: 2.2 million
Area: 105sq km (40.5sq miles)
GDP (Île de France): €572 billion
Highest elevation: Montmartre at 128m (420ft)
Mayor: Bertrand Delanoë (Socialist)
Divided into 20 *arrondissements*
Eiffel Tower: The tower has 2,500,000 rivets and is lit by 20,000 light bulbs

FLIGHT OF FANCY

The first manned flight took place in Paris when Pilatre de Rozier and the Marquis d'Arlandes made a 25-minute trip in a hot-air balloon from the Bois de Boulogne to what is now the 13th *arrondissement* on 21 November 1783. Among the crowd observing their feat was none other than Benjamin Franklin, one of the founding fathers of the USA.

CLOSED

Every Tuesday a crowd of disappointed tourists gathers outside the closed entrance to the Louvre pyramid. Remember that most major museums are closed one day a week: Monday for the city-run museums (such as Musée Carnavalet and Musée d'Art Moderne de la Ville de Paris) and Tuesday for national museums (including the Louvre, Centre Pompidou and Grand Palais).

DID YOU KNOW?

● Every evening, nearly 300 Parisian monuments, hotels, churches, fountains, bridges and canals are illuminated against the night sky.
● France has finally banned smoking inside restaurants, bars and cafés, for the dining pleasure of all.
● Watch your step! In spite of the city's best efforts to alleviate the problem, dog droppings are still a hazard.

Focus On Paris On Screen

Few places are as closely associated with film as Paris, the birthplace of cinema and a city whose many charms have been embedded in the world's imagination through the medium of the movies.

Birth of a New Medium

The history of modern cinema began properly in Paris on 28 December 1895, in the Salon Indien of the Grand Café on the boulevard des Capucines. At this venue, the Lumière brothers, Louis and Auguste, first demonstrated the potential of their invention, the *cinématographe*—a portable camera, film processing unit and projector combined—by screening 10 of their short films to a paying audience. The first film they showed was *La Sortie des Usines Lumière*, a simple shot of workers leaving the family's factory in Lyon. It lasted less than a minute, yet the public response was immediate and enthusiastic. A new entertainment medium had hit the scene, paving the way for one of the most influential and commercial forms of entertainment for future generations.

The Parisian Scene

Throughout cinema history, Paris itself has been one of the great stars of the silver screen. In the 1926 silent film *Paris*, Charles Ray fell for Joan Crawford in the louche setting of the Paris Apache (pronounced Ah-Pahsh) or demi-monde, the era of hedonistic lifestyles and decadent jazz clubs. The Apaches were originally Paris members of street gangs, and later the name was used for a new dance. In the 1950s, a string of big-budget Hollywood movies, from *An American in Paris* (1951) to *Funny Face* (1957), peddled the image of Paris as the capital of love and romance to a receptive international audience, with gamine European actresses like Leslie Caron and Audrey

Clockwise from top: La Pagode cinema in rue de Babylone; Le Champo cinema in rue des Écoles; a scene from An American in Paris, 1951; Les Deux

Hepburn personifying its elegance and fashion sense. In *Sabrina* (1954), Hepburn can be seen composing a letter to the wistful tune of *La Vie en Rose* as the Sacré Cœur is seen through an open window. The film and its content may only ever have been an outsider's ideal of the city of light, but as myths go it was a potent one. Hepburn was a Parisian *ingénue* in *Love in the Afternoon* (1957) and returned for *Paris When It Sizzles* (1964), though by then, perhaps, the formula had become a little stale.

Beyond the Romance
Inevitably, the depiction of Paris in French cinema has been somewhat less starry-eyed. Jean-Luc Godard's *Breathless* (*À bout de souffle*: 1959) may have had the relationship between Jean-Paul Belmondo and Jean Seberg at its core, but this *nouvelle vague* masterpiece is no sugar-coated romance. François Truffaut's *The Last Metro* (1980) dealt with the perils of the German occupation, Cyril Collard's *Savage Nights* (1992) with the complications of love in a time of AIDS. But French cinema is not immune to the capital's charms either, as Jean-Pierre Jeunet's magical, colour-saturated *Amélie* (2001) proved to huge international success. The film featured Audrey Tautou as a shy waitress in a Montmartre café and Paris itself— as enchanting as in any 1950s musical—was her co-star.

The Tradition Maintained
The city has remained true to its early passion for film. Director Luc Besson's project for a Cité Européenne du Cinéma (European City of Cinema) has brought 45,000sq m (484,200sq ft) of film production space in a former power station in the northern suburb of Saint-Denis, which opened in 2012. The impact of film on the city comes full circle.

Moulins café, setting for the film Amélie, 2001; *a poster for the Lumière brothers' new world of cinema; at work on* Paris When it Sizzles, 1964

Top Tips For...

These great suggestions will help you tailor your ideal visit to Paris, no matter how you choose to spend your time.

...Antiquing
Hunt for a bargain at the **Marché aux Puces de Saint-Ouen** (▷ 26–27), an immense weekend flea market.
Pick up a poster or etching by Toulouse-Lautrec at **Galerie Documents** (▷ 126).
Visit the warren of antiques shops at the **Louvre des Antiquaires** (▷ 127).

...Haute Couture
Find a wide selection of designer clothing at the department stores **Le Bon Marché Rive Gauche** (▷ 123), Galeries **Lafayette** or **Printemps** (▷ 126, panel).
Try on original yet timeless styles at **Colette** (▷ 124): it's cutting-edge and very exclusive.
Top off your look with one of **Marie Mercié's** fabulous hats (▷ 128).

...Fine Dining
Check out the two Michelin stars for **Gordon Ramsay au Trianon** (▷ 148), a luxurious dining experience on a trip to Versailles.
Find out how Guy Savoy turns cooking into an art form at his **eponymous restaurant** (▷ 149).
Dine at **Le Senderens**, the 2-star Michelin restaurant of Alain Senderens (▷ 150).

...All-Night Antics
Spot the celebs at trendy club **Le Baron** (▷ 135).
Drink martinis into the wee hours in the old-fashioned New World ambience of **Harry's New York Bar** (▷ 137).
Dance the night away at **Folie's Pigalle** (▷ 137).
Descend into the medieval basement at **Caveau de la Huchette** for high-ambience jazz (▷ 136).

Clockwise from top: A market stall at the Marché aux Puces de St-Ouen; relaxing in the Jardin du Luxembourg; admiring art in the Musée Carnavalet;

Take in a concert at the **Divan du Monde** (▷ 136) and stay on afterwards to hear some great guest DJs.

...Catering to the Kids
Ride the glass elevator to the top of the **Eiffel Tower** (▷ 60–61).
Explore interactive exhibitions at the **Cité des Sciences et de l'Industrie** in the Parc de la Villette (▷ 76).
Set the little darlings loose in the **Si Tu Veux** toy shop (▷ 129).

...Shoestring Pleasures
Take advantage of free admission to the permanent collections of all city-run museums: the **Musée Carnavalet** (▷ 28–29), **Musée d'Art Moderne de la Ville de Paris** (▷ 70) and many more.
Visit the **Atelier Brancusi**, a reconstruction of sculptor Constantin Brancusi's workshop, in front of the **Centre Georges Pompidou** (▷ 16–17), for free.

...Bird's-Eye Views
Stop shopping long enough to check out the view from **Printemps de la Maison's** ninth floor (▷ 126, panel).
See what the city looks like from central Paris's only skyscraper, the **Tour Montparnasse** (▷ 75).
Have a meal at the Eiffel Tower's **Le Jules Verne** restaurant (▷ 149) for superb food and spectacular views.

...Lazy Mornings
Cruise down the Seine in a *bateau mouche* (▷ 58–59).
Commune with the ghosts of Sartre and Hemingway at the **Café de Flore** (▷ 66).
Sit by the fountain in the **Jardin du Palais Royal** (▷ 69) with a book by Colette, who once lived there.

Harry's New York Bar in rue Daunou; the impressive glass dome of the prestigious Galeries Lafayette department store

Timeline

BEFORE 1000

● Celtic tribe of Parisii settles on Île de la Cité around 200BC.
● By AD100 the Roman city of Lutetia, later Paris, is growing fast.
● In 451 Sainte Geneviève saves Paris from the threat of Attila the Hun.

1163 The building of Notre-Dame starts.

1337–1453 Hundred Years War between France and England.

1431 Henry VI of England is crowned king of France in Notre-Dame.

1437 Charles VII regains control of Paris.

1572 St. Bartholomew Massacre occurs during Wars of Religion.

1682 Louis XIV and the court move to Versailles.

1700s Intellectuals, including Rousseau and Diderot, introduce radical new ideas during the Age of Enlightenment.

1789 Storming of the Bastille.

1792 Monarchy abolished; proclamation of the Republic.

1804 Napoleon crowned emperor.

1830 Bourbons overthrown; Louis-Philippe crowned.

1848 Revolution topples Louis-Philippe; Second Republic headed by Napoleon III, later crowned emperor.

REIGN OF TERROR

From 1793 to 1794 the Reign of Terror seized France, masterminded by the ruthless, power-crazed Jacobin leaders Robespierre and Danton. The king, Louis XVI, was convicted of treason and guillotined in January 1793, followed in October by his queen, Marie Antoinette. By mid-1794 more than 18,000 people are estimated to have been beheaded in France.

The gardens fronting the Château de Versailles

The Consecration of the Emperor Napoleon, by Jacques-Louis David

1852–70 Baron Haussmann oversees the transformation of Paris.

1870–71 Paris besieged by Prussians, civil uprising of the Commune, Republic restored.

1889 Eiffel Tower is completed.

1900 First Métro line opens.

1914–18 Paris bombarded by German cannon, Big Bertha.

1940 Nazis occupy Paris, followed by Liberation in 1944.

1958 De Gaulle heads Fifth Republic.

1977 Jacques Chirac is elected mayor (he becomes president in 1995). Centre Georges Pompidou opens.

1981 Election of President Mitterrand. He initiates his *Grands Projets*—a scheme of new building projects.

1999 December storms hit Paris; Versailles loses more than 10,000 trees.

2002 First *Paris Plage*, in which riverside roads are closed in summer to create an urban beach.

2007 Launch of Vélib', the city-wide bicycle hire scheme, with an on-street hire point every 300m (328 yards) across the city.

2011 The city adopts plans to improve the banks of the Seine, including partial closure to traffic.

The Liberation of Paris, 1944

THE SEINE

The city's history has been inextricably linked with the Seine since its earliest origins as a Gaulish village on the Île de la Cité, an islet in the river. The river represents the very lifeblood of Paris, flowing through its heart, animating the city, defining the capital geographically and reflecting its history in its many fine buildings. After centuries of pollution—when the river was used as a sewer—the Seine has been cleaned and its water is less polluted than it has been for years, although Jacques Chirac never swam in it as he promised he would before the end of his presidency.

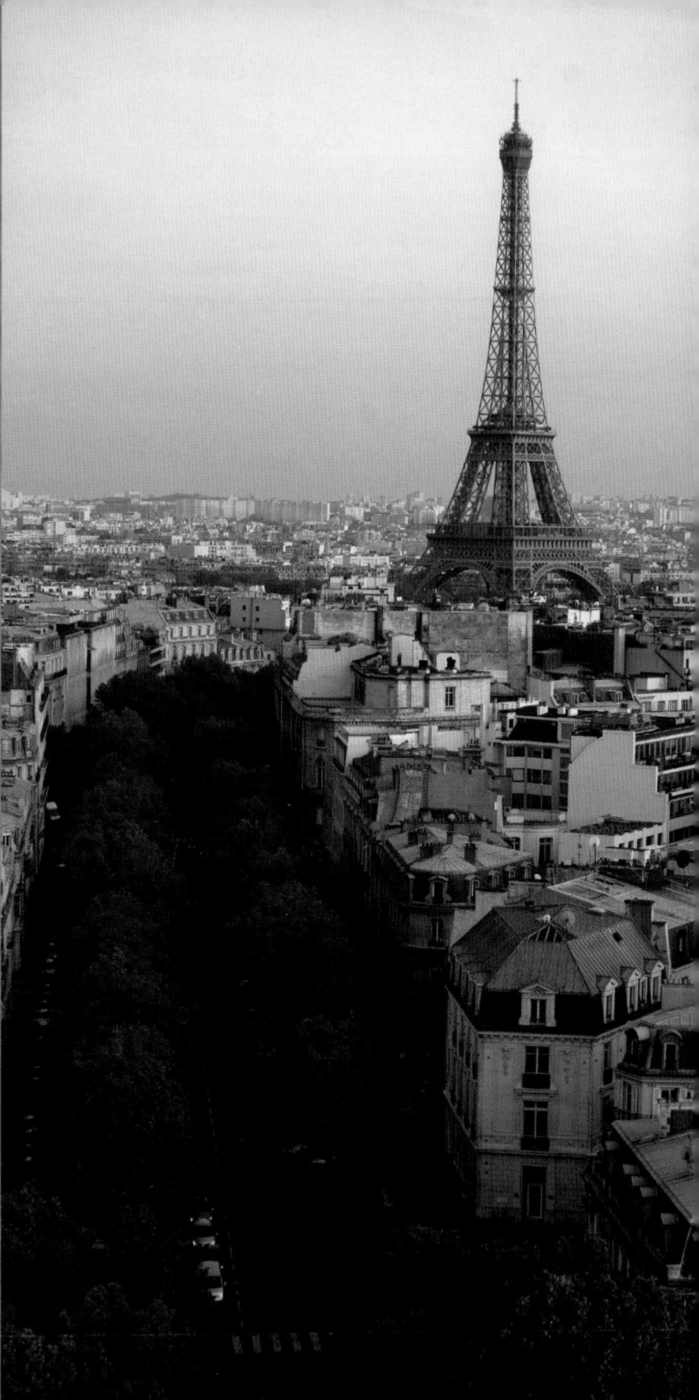

⭐ Top 25

This section contains the must-see Top 25 sights and experiences in Paris. They are listed alphabetically, and numbered so you can locate them on the inside front cover map.

HIGHLIGHTS

● Views from the terrace
● *La Marseillaise*, François Rude
● Tomb of the Unknown Soldier

TIP

● The museum has audio visual displays illustrating major historical events and the construction of the Arc.

At the hub of Haussmann's web of 12 avenues, which reach out like tentacles towards the city beyond, this is the ultimate symbol of Napoleon's military pretensions and might. Climb the 284 steps to the terrace for superb views.

National symbol Napoleon conceived the Arc de Triomphe as a symbol of his military might in 1806 but it was finished only in 1836 by Louis-Philippe. Two centuries on, the colossal monument is still an image of national pride. It plays a central role in many of France's key commemorations, including VE Day (8 May), Bastille Day (14 July) and Remembrance Day (11 November). Within its grounds are the Tomb of the Unknown Soldier, installed in 1921 after World War I, and a poignant Memorial

Clockwise from far left: The Arc de Triomphe at dusk; the Tomb of the Unknown Soldier beneath the monument; view of the Arc from the esplanade de la Défense; looking towards the Eiffel Tower; roll call of French generals, etched into the inside walls

Flame, added two years later. This flame is rekindled every evening.

Special interest There are wonderful views from the rooftop, 50m (164ft) high. From here you can admire Haussmann's weblike street design and look along the Grand Axis towards place de la Concorde in one direction and the Grande Arche in the other. There is a small shop and museum on the way up. At ground level, save time to admire the magnificent sculpted facade, the work of three artists. Don't miss the winged figure of Liberty on François Rude's sculpture *La Marseillaise*, calling the French to defend their nation (northeastern pillar, facing the Champs-Élysées). The 30 shields studding the crown of the arch each bear the name of a Revolutionary or Imperial victory.

THE BASICS

www.arc-de-triomphe.
monuments-nationaux.fr

🔛 B2

✉ Place Charles-de-Gaulle, 75008

☎ 01 55 37 73 77

🕐 Apr–Sep daily 10am–11pm; Oct–Mar 10am–10.30pm. Times may vary; last admission 30 minutes before closing

🚇 Charles de Gaulle-Étoile

♿ Moderate

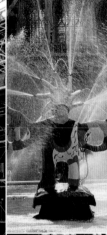

HIGHLIGHTS

● Design by Sir Richard Rogers, Renzo Piano and Jean-François Bodin
● View from the escalator
● Stravinsky fountain
● Trendy and cool design in Georges restaurant
● Avant-premières of new films and retrospectives of the work of famed directors in the cinema
● Design shop on level 1

TIP

● Queues for tickets can be long; cut waiting times by booking in advance online.

Late opening hours make an exhibition visit possible between an *apéritif* and dinner in this still-controversial cultural area. You can take your pick between the genesis of modernism, an art film or a drama performance.

High-tech culture More than a mere landmark in the extensive facelift that Paris has undergone since the 1970s, the high-tech Centre Pompidou (known to Parisians as Beaubourg) is a hive of changing cultural activity. Contemporary art, architecture, design, photography, theatre, cinema and dance are all represented, while the lofty structure offers exceptional views over central Paris. Take the transparent escalator tubes for a bird's-eye view of the piazza, where jugglers, artists, musicians and portrait artists perform for the crowds.

Clockwise from far left: Inside-out exterior of the building; detail of the Stravinsky fountain outside the Centre; futuristic features on the exterior; glass corridor with fine views over the city; the Centre viewed above the rooftops of the city; more pipes and structures on the facade of the Centre

Classic modernism The permanent collections of the Musée National d'Art Moderne feature work from 1905 to the 1960s on the fifth floor with exhibitions of works from the contemporary collection on level four. Items from the 59,000-strong collection are changed regularly and range from Cubism by Georges Braque to Pop Art by Andy Warhol and video art by Korean artist Nam June Paik. For a chronological overview start on the fifth floor. Levels 1, 4 and 6 are for temporary exhibitions, while a public information library is on levels 1, 2 and 3. The ground level includes a bookshop and museum boutique (there are other bookstands on levels 4 and 6), a post office and a children's workshop. There are cinemas on the first and lower floors and the restaurant Georges, with its wonderful views over the city, is on the top floor.

THE BASICS

www.centrepompidou.fr

➕ K5

✉ Place Georges-Pompidou, 75004

☎ 01 44 78 12 33

🎫 Museum and exhibits Wed–Mon 11–10 (last tickets 8); Atelier Brancusi (▷ 9) Wed–Mon 2–6; Library Mon, Wed–Fri 12–10, Sat–Sun 11–10

🍴 Georges restaurant on 6th floor (▷ 148); café on mezzanine

🚇 Rambuteau, Hôtel de Ville

🚌 38, 47, 67, 75, 76

🚆 RER Line A, B, Châtelet-Les Halles

♿ Excellent

💰 Expensive

- Marie Antoinette's cell
- Tour Bonbec
- Prisoners' cells upstairs

TIP

● If you also plan to visit Sainte-Chapelle (▷ 56–57), go to the Conciergerie first and buy a joint ticket, to avoid the queues at Sainte-Chapelle. But do try to get to Sainte-Chapelle in the morning, before it gets very busy.

The ghosts of the victims of the guillotine must surely haunt this stark and gloomy place that served as a prison and torture chamber for more than five centuries and remains full of macabre mementoes of its grisly past.

From palace to prison Rising over the Seine in menacing grandeur, the Conciergerie was built from 1299 to 1313 as part of a royal complex that also included Sainte-Chapelle. From 1391 until 1914 the building functioned as a prison and torture chamber, its reputation striking fear in the population. During the Revolution more than 2,700 people appeared before the Revolutionary Tribunal at the Conciergerie, including Marie Antoinette and Maximilien Robespierre.

Clockwise from top left: The beautiful Conciergerie graces the banks of the Seine; detail of the building flanked by trees; the impressive clock on the Tour de l'Horloge; representation of the clerk's room; the moody lighting enhances the Salle des Gens d'Armes

Relive history The boulevard du Palais entrance takes you into the hauntingly lit Salle des Gens d'Armes. This rib-vaulted hall is considered one of the finest examples of secular Gothic architecture in Europe. The curious spiral staircase on the right of the hall once led to the Great Ceremonial Hall on the upper floor of the palace. Off the Salle des Gens d'Armes is the gloomy Salle des Gardes; this acted as an antechamber to the now-vanished Grand' chambre on the upper floor, where the Revolutionary Tribunal sat in 1793. Across the corridor known as the rue de Paris is the Galerie des Prisonniers, where lawyers, prisoners and visitors mingled. Here is a re-creation of the concierge's and clerk's offices, as well as the Salle de Toilette, where prisoners were prepared for execution. At the far end is a poignant re-creation of Marie Antoinette's cell.

THE BASICS

www.conciergerie.
monuments-nationaux.fr

➕ J6

✉ 2 boulevard du Palais, Île de la Cité, 75001

☎ 01 53 40 60 80

🕐 Daily 9.30–6; times may vary

🚇 Cité, Châtelet

🚌 21, 24, 27, 38, 58, 81, 85 and Balabus

🎫 Moderate (joint ticket with Sainte-Chapelle expensive)

❓ Guided tours by appointment

4 Galerie Vivienne and the Passages Couverts

HIGHLIGHTS

● Mosaic floor, Galerie Vivienne
● Stamp dealers
● M. G. Segas
● Vintage children's books
● Décor, Le Grand Colbert

Centred on the 2nd *arrondissement* is a hidden network of interconnecting 19th-century shopping arcades or *passages couverts* that enable you to stroll under cover most of the way from the Palais Royal to the Grands Boulevards and beyond.

Galerie Vivienne Between the late 18th and early 19th centuries the Right Bank included a network of 140 covered passageways—the fashionable shopping malls of the time. Of those that survive, the Galerie Vivienne (1823) is perhaps the most glamorous, squeezed in between the Bibliothèque Nationale and the place des Victoires. You can track down designer clothes—Jean-Paul Gaultier was one of the first to open a shop here—or shop for intriguing toys. It's perfect for a rainy day.

Clockwise from far left: Style and elegance feature in the Galerie Vivienne; taking a break in the café; the elaborate entrance; a superb ornate clock embellishes the wall; a nod to the present with this modern sign at the Galerie

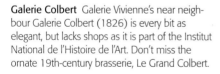

Galerie Colbert Galerie Vivienne's near neighbour Galerie Colbert (1826) is every bit as elegant, but lacks shops as it is part of the Institut National de l'Histoire de l'Art. Don't miss the ornate 19th-century brasserie, Le Grand Colbert.

More offbeat browsing These interlinked arcades thread their way north from rue Saint-Marc across the boulevard de Montmartre and into the 9th *arrondissement*. The labyrinthine Passage des Panoramas (1800) is a little down-at-heel in places but full of inexpensive restaurants and stamp dealers. Facing it across boulevard de Montmartre is the Passage Jouffroy (1845), where the quirkiest of the boutiques is M. G. Segas, which sells antique walking canes. Further north still, the quieter Passage Verdeau (1847) features vintage book dealers.

THE BASICS

www.galerie-vivienne.com
www.passagedes
panoramas.fr
www.passagejouffroy.com
✚ H4–H3
✉ Galerie Vivienne: 4 rue des Petits-Champs/6 rue Vivienne, 75002.
Passage des Panoramas:
10 rue Saint-Marc, 75002
🚇 Bourse, Palais-Royal, Grands Boulevards
🚌 20, 39, 74, 85
♿ Good
👆 Free

21

5 Jardin du Luxembourg

HIGHLIGHTS

- Médicis fountain
- Musée du Luxembourg
- Bandstand
- Statue of Delacroix
- Orangerie
- Experimental orchard
- Beekeeping school
- Statues of queens of France

Despite the crowds, these gardens are serene in all weathers and are the epitome of French landscaping. This idealized image of an unhurried Parisian existence is far from the daily truth of noise and traffic.

Layout Radiating from the large octagonal pond in front of the Palais du Luxembourg (now the Senate) are terraces, paths and a wide tree-lined alley that leads down to the Observatory crossroads. Natural attractions include shady chestnuts, potted orange and palm trees, an orchard and tropical hothouses. Statues of the queens of France and artists and writers are dotted about.

Park activities All year round joggers pound the circumference and in summer sunbathers

Clockwise from far left: Strolling in front of the Palais du Luxembourg; detail of the Médicis fountain; relaxing in the gardens; bronze statue, l'Acteur Grec, by Charles-Arthur Bourgeois; the gardens provide the perfect setting for a game of chess

and bookworms settle into park chairs, card- and chess-players claim the shade in front of the Orangerie, bands tune up at the bandstand near the boulevard Saint-Michel entrance and children burn off energy on swings and donkey rides. Fountains, tennis courts, beehives, a puppet theatre and children's playgrounds offer other distractions. In the northwest corner of the park is Paris's oldest public museum, the Musée du Luxembourg. Opened in 1750, it became the first contemporary art museum in 1818 and today stages important temporary exhibitions of art.

Inspiration The Palais du Luxembourg and gardens were commissioned by Marie de Médicis, wife of Henri IV, in 1615, and designed to resemble her childhood Florentine home.

THE BASICS

🚆 G8/H8

✉ Main entrance place Edmond Rostand, 75006

☎ Park 01 42 34 23 89. Musée du Luxembourg 01 40 13 62 00; www. museeduluxembourg.fr

🕐 Park daylight hours. Museum daily 10–7.30 (10pm Mon and Fri)

🍴 Open-air café, kiosk

Ⓜ Odéon

🚉 RER Line B, Luxembourg

🚌 58, 63, 70, 84, 86, 89, 93 (to museum)

♿ Very good

💷 Park free; museum expensive

HIGHLIGHTS

- Jeu de Paume
- Orangerie
- Outdoor sculptures
- Views

Tucked between the River Seine and the rue de Rivoli, the Tuileries is not the most peaceful park in Paris, but being so central it is easily one of the most visited. It's very much an urban park, with the noise of the traffic hard to escape, but it is still a popular place for locals to take a break, and where children can play.

Good views It's also a place from where visitors can see several of the city's main attractions. There are good views of the Louvre, the Eiffel Tower, the Musée d'Orsay across the river and up to the Arc de Triomphe standing at the top of the Champs-Élysées.

Design The formal design of the gardens can be credited to the landscape architect André le

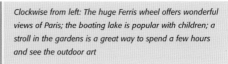

Clockwise from left: The huge Ferris wheel offers wonderful views of Paris; the boating lake is popular with children; a stroll in the gardens is a great way to spend a few hours and see the outdoor art

Nôtre, who was gardener to King Louis XIV and the man responsible for the spectacular gardens at Versailles. Le Nôtre laid out the Tuileries in 1664, and over 300 years later they are still being enjoyed.

Activities In one corner is a boating pond, and at the opposite end, overlooking the place de la Concorde, are two of the city's finest small galleries, the Orangerie (▷ 51) and the Jeu de Paume (▷ 51). The latter gets its name from the fact that it was once a real tennis court (*jeu de paume*) and the former a warm winter home for the orange trees from the Jardin. There is plenty of outdoor art in the gardens, too. Works by Giacometti, Rodin and Henry Moore are on display, and several bronzes by Aristide Maillol.

THE BASICS

➕ F4–5/G4–5
✉ 113 rue de Rivoli, 75001
🕓 Jun–Aug daily 7am–11pm; Apr–May, Sep 7am–9pm; Oct–Mar 7.30–7.30
🍴 Cafés
🚇 Tuileries
♿ Good
✋ Free

HIGHLIGHTS

● Marché Serpette: art, high-quality furniture
● Marché Paul Bert: trendy items, including classic modern furniture
● Marché Jules Vallès: bric-a-brac
● Marché Biron: antiques, glass, art deco

TIP

● The market area is very extensive, so pick up a free map from the tourist office at 7 impasse Simon by the Marché Paul Bert.

A Sunday pastime popular with many locals is to look for bargains at the city's flea markets, of which the *crème de la crème* is still this one. Nowhere else will you find such a fascinating cross-section of Parisian society.

Duck and banter The approach from the Métro station to this sprawling 7ha (17-acre) market is uninspiring as it entails bypassing jeans and sportswear stalls before ducking under the Périphérique overpass and finally entering the fray. Persevere and you may discover an antique gem, a fake or a second-hand item. If your budget won't stretch to that you can choose an old postcard of Paris from the thousands on show. Everything and anything is displayed here and all commerce is carried on in the true bantering style of the *faubourgs*.

Clockwise from far left: Antiques and curiosities at the market; browse the books at Zoppa & Zoppa; pretty antique basin for sale; collector's items include an array of soda siphons; intricate carving is a feature of French furniture

It pays to get 'creatively lost', since the most intriguing vendors are not necessarily the ones with the most prominent sites. In particular, don't miss the upper level if you're visiting the Marché Dauphine.

Bargain Registered dealers are divided into more than a dozen official markets, which interconnect through bustling passageways. Along the fringes are countless hopefuls who set up temporary stands to sell goods ranging from obsolete kitchenware to old jukeboxes and junk. Although unashamedly a tourist trap, there is something for everyone here, but do go early. Bargaining is obligatory. Stop for lunch in one of the bistros along the rue des Rosiers or try the terrace of the café-theatre A Picolo at 58 rue Jules-Vallès, which has occasional jazz concerts.

THE BASICS

www.marchesauxpuces.fr
✚ Off map
✉ Porte de Clignancourt, 75018
☎ 01 58 61 22 90
🕐 Sat 9–6, Sun 10–6, Mon 11–5 (reduced hours in Aug)
🍴 Cafés and restaurants on rue des Rosiers
🚇 Porte de Clignancourt
🚌 56, 60, 85, 95, 137, 166, 255
♿ Good
💷 Free
❓ Beware of pickpockets

There is no better museum than this to plunge you into the history of Paris, and its renovated mansion setting is hard to beat. Period rooms, objects, documents and paintings combine to illustrate the city's turbulent past.

Ornamental excess This captivating collection is displayed within adjoining 16th- and 17th-century town houses. The main entrance is through the superb courtyard of the Hôtel Carnavalet (1548), once the home of the celebrated writer Madame de Sévigné. Here attention focuses on the Middle Ages, the Renaissance and the decorative excess reached under Louis XIV, Louis XV and Louis XVI. Some of the richly painted and sculpted interiors are original to the building; others, such as the

Clockwise from far left: The magnificent entrance to the Hôtel Carnavalet, now home to the museum; art and architecture inside the museum; George Fouquet's jewellery boutique designed by Alphonse Mucha; splendid topiary in the museum gardens

wood panels from the Hôtel Colbert de Villacerf and Brunetti's trompe-l'œil staircase paintings, have been brought in.

Revolution to the present Next door, the well-renovated Hôtel Le Peletier de Saint-Fargeau (1688) exhibits remarkable objects from the Revolution—a period when anything and everything was emblazoned with slogans—and continues with Napoleon I's reign, the Restoration, the Second Empire, the Commune and finally the Belle Époque. Figures such as Robespierre and Madame de Récamier come to life within their chronological context. The collection ends in the early 20th century with fine reconstructions of interiors, including the bedroom of Marcel Proust, who, owing to severe asthma, was often confined to bed.

THE BASICS

www.carnavalet.paris.fr

⊞ L6

✉ 23 rue de Sévigné, 75003

☎ 01 44 59 58 58

🕐 Tue–Sat 10–6

Ⓢ Saint-Paul

🚌 29, 69, 76, 96

♿ Carnavalet: few; Le Peletier: good

💶 Free; temporary exhibitions moderate

9 Musée du Louvre

- Palace of Khorsabad
- Glass pyramid entrance, designed by I. M. Pei
- *Bataille de San Romano*, Uccello
- *Mona Lisa*, da Vinci
- Napoleon III apartments
- Vénus de Milo
- Cour Carrée at night
- The Marly Horses

TIP

- To avoid the crowds, visit early morning or Wednesday or Friday evening.

Nocturnal lighting transforms the Louvre's glass pyramid entrance into a gigantic cut diamond—just a foretaste of the treasures contained within.

The world's largest museum Since 1981 the Louvre has undergone a radical transformation including moving the museum's star attraction, the *Mona Lisa*, which was relocated to a room specially refurbished to make viewing the painting easier. Originally a medieval fortress, the Louvre first took shape as a private art gallery under François I, eager to display his Italian loot. Henri IV added several galleries, completed in 1610. After escaping the excesses of the Revolutionary mob, in 1793 it became a people's museum and was later enlarged by Napoleon I, who enriched its collection.

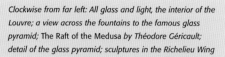

Clockwise from far left: All glass and light, the interior of the Louvre; a view across the fountains to the famous glass pyramid; The Raft of the Medusa by Théodore Géricault; detail of the glass pyramid; sculptures in the Richelieu Wing

Art fortress The vast collection of some 35,000 exhibits is arranged on four floors of three wings: Sully (east), Richelieu (north) and Denon (south), while beneath the elegant Cour Carrée lies the keep of the original medieval fortress. A new home for the Islamic art collection opened in the Cours Visconti in 2012, and displays some 2,000 objects from three continents. Almost 5,000 years of art are covered at the museum, starting with Egyptian antiquities and culminating with European painting up to 1848.

Making the most of your visit There is no way that you'll be able to see everything in one visit, so you'll need to be selective. The free museum map, available from the information desk, also highlights the key works.

THE BASICS

www.louvre.fr

➕ H5

✉ 99 rue de Rivoli, 75058. Enter via Pyramid or Carrousel

☎ 01 40 20 50 50; Auditorium 01 40 20 55 55

🕐 Wed–Mon 9–6 (until 9.45pm Wed, Fri)

🍴 Restaurants and cafés

🚇 Palais-Royal–Musée du Louvre

🚌 21, 24, 27, 39, 48, 68, 69, 72, 81, 95

♿ Excellent

💰 Moderate; temporary exhibitions expensive; free first Sun of every month

❓ Tours, audioguides, lectures, films, workshops, concerts. Buy your ticket online to save a long wait

HIGHLIGHTS

- *Impression—soleil levant*, Monet
- Gold table-tray
- *Promenade près d'Argenteuil*, Monet
- *Charing Cross Bridge*, Monet
- *L'Allée des Rosiers*, Monet
- *Le Pont Japonais*, Monet
- Monet's *Water Lilies* series
- Monet's spectacles

The Marmottan Monet Museum is in the residential 16th *arrondissement*, where a mesmerizing collection of Monet paintings makes for a vibrant escape from the urban aspects of Paris life.

Rich donations This often overlooked treasure of Parisian culture offers an eclectic collection built up over the years from the original donation of Renaissance and First Empire paintings and furniture bequeathed by the art historian Paul Marmottan in 1932. His elegant 19th-century mansion, furnished with Renaissance tapestries and sculptures and Napoleonic furniture, was later given an extra boost by the stunning Wildenstein collection of 313 pages from illustrated manuscripts from the 13th to the 16th centuries, as well as an exceptional

Far left and below: An elegant room used to display Impressionist paintings; plenty of space to fully appreciate the works of Claude Monet and his contemporaries

donation from Michel Monet of works by his father Claude, the Impressionist painter. Other generous donations include works by Monet's contemporaries Gauguin, Renoir, Boudin, Pissarro, Sisley, Berthe Morisot and Gustave Caillebotte, but it is Monet's canvases of dappled irises, wisteria and water lilies, from his last years at Giverny, that are among the most sought out and memorable.

Visiting the museum The museum shop and Salons Impressionnistes are on the ground floor. You will find more Impressionists and the Salle Monet in the basement, while the upper floor hosts the Wildenstein collection of illuminated manuscripts. The museum also stages regular temporary exhibitions on themes related to its collections.

THE BASICS

www.marmottan.com
➕ Off map
✉ 2 rue Louis-Boilly, 75016
☎ 01 44 96 50 33
🕐 Tue–Sun 10–6 (Thu until 8)
🚇 La Muette
🚌 22, 32, 52, 63
🚉 RER Line C, Boulainvilliers
♿ Moderate

HIGHLIGHTS

- *La Dame à la Licorne (The Lady and the Unicorn)* tapestries
- Gold altar frontal
- *Pilier des Nautes*
- Stone heads from Notre-Dame
- Medieval gardens
- Seventh-century votive crown
- Stained glass
- Abbot's Chapel

Take a deep breath outside this museum, surrounded by re-created medieval gardens, and prepare to enter a time warp in which the days of troubadours and courtly love are conjured up.

Treasures The Gothic turreted Hôtel de Cluny was built at the end of the 15th century by Abbot Jacques d'Amboise and is one of France's finest examples of domestic architecture of this period. The museum it houses, also known as the Musée de Cluny, has 23,000 objects in its collection, most amassed by Alexandre du Sommerard, a 19th-century medievalist. The most famous exhibits are the beautiful *La Dame à la Licorne* tapestries (late 15th century). Costumes, accessories, textiles and tapestries are of Byzantine, Coptic or European

Clockwise from far left: Stone staircase, bathed in lights, in the Gothic Hôtel de Cluny; exterior of the building, now housing the museum; detail of a religious painting displayed in the museum; exterior courtyard, once the site of ancient Roman baths; detail of shells on exterior

origin, while the gold and metalwork room has outstanding pieces of Gallic, Barbarian, Merovingian and Visigothic artistry. Room VIII houses 21 stone heads knocked from statues on the west front of Notre-Dame. Stained glass, table games, ceramics, wood carvings, illuminated manuscripts and Books of Hours, altarpieces and religious statuary complete this exceptional display.

Baths The late-Roman baths of Lutetia, comprised of cold (frigidarium), tepid (tepidarium) and hot (caldarium) rooms, form part of the museum complex. The most substantial surviving element is the frigidarium, whose recently restored 14.7m (48ft) vaulted ceiling makes it one of the most important structures from antiquity to survive north of the Loire.

THE BASICS

www.musee-moyenage.fr

➕ J7

✉ 6 place Paul-Painlevé, 75005

☎ 01 53 73 78 00

🕐 Wed–Mon 9.15–5.45; last admission 30 minutes before closing

Ⓜ Cluny-La Sorbonne

🚌 21, 27, 38, 63, 85, 86, 87

🚆 RER Line B, Cluny

💰 Moderate; free first Sun of every month

❓ Guided tours of vaults, baths and collections in English: call ahead

You'll either love or hate the conversion of this 1900 train station. But whatever your view, its art collections, covering the years from 1848 to 1914, are a must for anyone interested in this crucial art period.

Monolithic When this museum finally opened in 1986 controversy ran high: Gae Aulenti's heavy stone structures lay unhappily under Laloux's delicate iron-and-glass shell, built as a train terminus in 1900. But the collections redeem this faux pas, offering a solid overview of the momentous period from Romanticism to Fauvism. Works by the giants of French art—Degas, Monet, Cézanne, Van Gogh, Renoir, Sisley and Pissarro—are the biggest crowd pullers. The opulent restaurant of the old Hôtel d'Orsay on the first floor is a grand setting.

TIP

● A Paris Museum Pass (▷ 170) allows you to skip the queues for tickets.

Clockwise from far left: Check out the view through the giant clock in the museum's café; plenty of Monet's paintings are on show; memories of a train station are evoked on the vast ground floor; the ornate station clock; the Musée d'Orsay sits elegantly along the River Seine

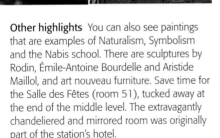

Other highlights You can also see paintings that are examples of Naturalism, Symbolism and the Nabis school. There are sculptures by Rodin, Émile-Antoine Bourdelle and Aristide Maillol, and art nouveau furniture. Save time for the Salle des Fêtes (room 51), tucked away at the end of the middle level. The extravagantly chandeliered and mirrored room was originally part of the station's hotel.

All change Since 2009, extensive renovation work has enlarged the exhibition area and improved lighting. The new home for the Impressionist works is a refurbished, top-lit space on the fifth floor, with the post-Impressionists on the middle level on the rue de Lille side of the museum. The new displays will aid the flow of visitors.

THE BASICS

www.musee-orsay.fr
✚ F5
✉ 62 rue de Lille, 75007
☎ 01 40 49 48 00 or 01 40 49 48 14
🕐 Tue–Sun 9.30–6, Thu 9.30am–9.45pm
🍽 Restaurant on first floor; Café du Lion near museum entrance
Ⓜ Solférino
🚌 24, 63, 68, 69, 73, 83, 84, 94
🚆 RER Line C, Musée d'Orsay
♿ Excellent
💶 Moderate; free first Sun of each month
❓ Audio and guided tours, concerts and lectures

★13 Musée Picasso

HIGHLIGHTS

● Ceramics
● *Man with a Guitar*
● Studies for *Les Demoiselles d'Avignon*

TIP

● Until the museum reopens, you can get the latest information and see a model of the renovations opposite the museum entrance (Tue–Sat 1–6pm).

The Picasso Museum already housed the largest collection of works by Picasso in the world, before it closed for a $62 million facelift. It promises even more works on display when it re-opens in spring 2014.

Taxes After Picasso died in 1973, his family owed about $50 million in death duties. In lieu of this they gave the state 203 of Picasso's paintings, 158 sculptures, and many other items including curios he had collected and paintings by other artists. When his widow died in 1986, further works were handed over. The result was the basis of this remarkable collection covering all periods of the artist's life.

Hôtel Salé The building itself is a delight, originally built in the 1650s by a man who

Clockwise from far left: The elegant interior of the Musée Picasso; museum sign; ornate detail on the Hôtel Salé, a fiting home for the artist's works; the Hôtel Salé illuminated at night

gained his own wealth from collecting the very unpopular salt tax that was levied in France at the time. It later became an embassy, and a school, and was acquired by the French state in 1964. Four years later it was declared a historic monument, and it opened as the Musée Picasso in 1985.

The collection Spread over three floors, the collection does not contain the artist's best-known works, like *Guernica*, but its delight is that it shows many works that he wanted to keep for himself. After all, he once declared himself the greatest collector of Picassos in the world, and here you will see beautiful examples of his very varied work from his Blue Period, cubism, surrealism, and others showing the astonishing range of his talents.

THE BASICS

www.musee-picasso.fr
➕ L5
✉ Hôtel Salé, 5 rue de Thorigny, 75003
☎ 01 42 71 25 21
🕐 Closed till spring 2014; see website for latest information
🍴 See website for latest information
Ⓜ Saint-Paul, Saint-Sébastien-Froissart
♿ Very good
ℹ See website for latest information

14 Musée du quai Branly

- A glass tower of 9,000 musical instruments
- Nepalese ritual lamp
- Aztec statues
- The Harter bequest of masks and sculptures from the Cameroon

TIP

- The museum gardens are particularly magical in the evening, when they are beautifully illuminated.

This very eye-catching museum, near the Seine and Eiffel Tower, is dedicated to the cultural heritage of Africa, Asia, Oceania and the Americas.

A 21st-century venue Built on five levels and crowned by a wide terrace with fine views of the Eiffel Tower, the museum is hidden from view by trees and thick vegetation. *Le mur végétal* (plant wall) festoons the north facade, with 15,000 plants representing 150 species from all over the world.

Inside A swooping white ramp leads through a dark tunnel before reaching the display area, where you are greeted by a 10th-century anthropomorphic Dogon wood statue from Mali, its one remaining arm reaching skywards.

Clockwise from far left: Covered in indigenous plants, the exterior of the museum; head of a figurine from Ifa, Nigeria, dating from 12th–14th century; Oceania Gallery; Uli wooden sculpture, 18th–early 19th century, from New Ireland, Oceania

This splendid beginning sets the tone for other highlights, including painted animal hides from the Americas, decorated with battle scenes and abstract earth and sky motifs; a glass tower of a large number of musical instruments that have been gathered from all corners of the world; and a headdress from Malekula Island, worn by dancers during rituals in the early 20th century. To aid navigation through the museum, each of the different regions has its own floor colouring.

Other attractions Several temporary exhibitions are staged each year. There's also drama, dance and music in the theatre. The museum organizes debates on historic and contemporary issues. There is also a cinema, plus regular hands-on workshops for adults and children from three years of age.

THE BASICS

www.quaibranly.fr

➕ B5

✉ 22 rue de l'Université, 75007

☎ 01 56 61 70 00

🕐 Sun, Tue–Wed 11–7, Thu–Sat 11–9

🍴 Gourmet restaurant Les Ombres on the roof terrace (01 47 53 68 00) and Café Branly in the garden

Ⓜ Alma-Marceau

🚌 42, 63, 72, 80, 92

🚆 RER line C, Pont de l'Alma

♿ Good

🎫 Moderate; gardens free

HIGHLIGHTS

- *Les Bourgeois de Calais*
  (The Burghers of Calais)
- *Le Penseur (The Thinker)*
- *La Porte de l'Enfer*
  (The Gates of Hell)
- *Le Baiser (The Kiss)*
- *La Main de Dieu*
  (The Hand of God)
- *Adam et Eve*
- *Ugolin*
- *Le Père Tanguy*, Van
  Gogh
- Original staircase

As an antidote to the military might of
Les Invalides (▷ 68–69), wander into the
enchanting Musée Rodin, which is often
forgotten by Parisians.

Hard times The rococo Hôtel Biron, which
houses the museum, was built for a wig-maker
in 1730 and has an interesting history. One
owner (the Duc de Lauzun) was sent to the
guillotine and the house has been used succes-
sively as a dance hall, convent, school and
artists' studios. Rodin lived here from 1908 until
his death in 1917. In 1919 the house became
a museum. The renovated chapel in the
grounds is now used for temporary exhibitions.

Sculpture The elegant, luminous interior
houses the collection that Rodin left to the

Clockwise from far left: The most famous Rodin sculpture, The Thinker, in the garden of the museum; the facade of the museum; Rodin sculptures around the gardens; detail from The Burghers of Calais sculpture; the former Hôtel Biron, now housing the museum; more sculptures inside

nation. It ranges from his early sketches to the later watercolours and includes many of his most celebrated white marble and bronze sculptures, including *The Kiss (Le Baiser)*. There are busts of the composer Mahler and writer Victor Hugo, among others, and a series of studies of Balzac. Alongside the Rodins are works by his contemporaries, in particular his tragic mistress and model, Camille Claudel, as well as Eugène Carrière, Edvard Munch, Renoir, Monet and Van Gogh. Rodin's furniture and antiques complete this exceptional collection.

Retreat The museum's private gardens are Paris's third largest and contain several major sculptures, a pond, flowering shrubs and benches for a quiet read. It's worth buying the garden-only ticket just for a respite from city life.

THE BASICS

www.musee-rodin.fr

➕ E6

✉ 79 rue de Varenne, 75007

☎ 01 44 18 61 10

🕐 Tue–Sun 10–5.45; last admission 5.15. Garden closes Apr–Sep 6pm; Oct–Mar 5pm

🍴 Peaceful garden café

Ⓜ Varenne, Invalides

🚌 69, 82, 87, 92

Ⓡ RER line C, Invalides

♿ Wheelchair access

💰 Moderate; garden inexpensive

TOP 25

HIGHLIGHTS

● Views from the towers
● Rose windows
● Portals
● Flying buttresses
● The gargoyles
● Emmanuel bell
● Organ
● *Pietà*, Coustou
● Statue of Notre-Dame de Paris (14th-century Virgin and Child)

TIP

● Try to visit just before a service to experience the sense of anticipation as lights are turned on and people gather to worship.

Spectacular is the word to describe this extraordinary monument, with its 93m (305ft) spire and world-renowned flying buttresses. One of the finest views of the cathedral is from the *quais* to the east.

Evolution Construction started in 1163 and didn't finish until 1345. Since then the cathedral has suffered from pollution, politics, aesthetic trends and religious change. Most of the stained-glass windows were replaced with clear glass (the stained glass was later restored) in the 18th century, while Revolutionary anti-clericalism toppled statues and the spire was taken down. Not least, Viollet-le-Duc, the fervent 19th-century medievalist architect, was let loose on its restoration and initiated radical alterations.

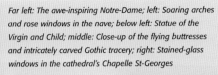
Far left: The awe-inspiring Notre-Dame; left: Soaring arches and rose windows in the nave; below left: Statue of the Virgin and Child; middle: Close-up of the flying buttresses and intricately carved Gothic tracery; right: Stained-glass windows in the cathedral's Chapelle St-Georges

Interior grandeur The hushed, softly lit stone interior contains numerous chapels, tombs and statues. The sacristy on the south side of the choir is where the treasure of Notre-Dame is kept: medieval manuscripts, religious parapher-nalia and relics, including the Crown of Thorns. Look at the magnificent stained glass above the mighty organ, one of the largest in Europe. The Crypt is often overlooked because its entrance is outside, but you can see Roman foundations and archaeological finds down there. Climb the towers (422 steps; no elevator) for fantastic views and a close-up of the gargoyles. Look closely at the three asymmetrical sculpted portals on the facade: These once served as a Bible for illiterate worshippers. Finally, walk round the cathedral for a view of its extravagant flying buttresses.

THE BASICS

www.notredamedeparis.fr

🞹 J7

✉ Place du Parvis Notre-Dame–Place Jean-Paul II, 75004

☎ 01 42 34 56 10
Crypt 01 55 42 50 10

🕐 Cathedral Mon–Fri 8–6.45, Sat, Sun 8–7.15. Towers Jun–Aug daily 10–6.30, until 11 Sat–Sun; Apr–May, Sep 10–6.30; Oct–Mar 10–5.30

🚇 Cité, Saint-Michel

🚌 21, 24, 38, 47, 85, 96

🚊 RER Lines B and C, Saint-Michel

♿ Good (not in towers)

💶 Cathedral free; tower and crypt moderate; treasury inexpensive

HIGHLIGHTS

● Grand Staircase
● Grand Foyer
● Auditorium
● Facade
● The shop, Galerie de l'Opéra de Paris (▷ 126)

This is an ornate wedding cake of a building, but the sumptuous and riotous details that decorate its every surface are in fact the perfect epitaph to the frenetic architectural activities of France's Second Empire.

Past glory When Charles Garnier's opera house was inaugurated in 1875 it marked the end of Haussmann's ambitious urban facelift and announced the sociocultural movement to the Belle Époque, with Nijinksy and Diaghilev's Ballets Russes as later highlights. The opera house, together with a fatal accident wth a chandelier in 1896, was the inspiration for the novel *The Phantom of the Opera* (1910) by Gaston Leroux. Today the Salle Garnier stages both dance and opera. Rudolf Nureyev was director of the Paris Ballet here between 1983 and 1989.

Left: The ornate facade of the Palais Garnier; middle: One of Carrier-Belleuse's lamp-bearing statues; right: The gilded statue of Poetry *on the roof of the building*

Dazzle The Palais Garnier's extravagant, regilded facade of arches, winged horses, friezes, columns, lamps and much statuary is topped by a verdigris dome and leads into a majestic foyer. This is dominated by the Grand Staircase, dripping with balconies and chandeliers, in turn sweeping upwards to the Grand Foyer and its gilded mirrors, marble, murals and Murano glass. Don't miss the equally ornate auditorium, with its dazzling gold-leaf decorations and red-velvet seats, and Marc Chagall's incongruous and, at the time in 1964, controversial ceiling. The auditorium can be visited except during rehearsals. The opera house also has a library and a museum of operatic memorabilia. The building's renovation has removed the layer of black soot that used to cover it, leaving it simply resplendent.

THE BASICS

www.operadeparis.fr

✚ G3

✉ Place de l'Opéra, 75009

☎ Information, reservations 0892 89 90 90 (34¢ per min)

🕐 Daily 10–4.30 (times can vary)

🍴 Bar open during shows

Ⓜ Opéra

🚌 20, 21, 22, 27, 29, 42, 52, 53, 66, 68, 81, 95

🚆 RER Line A, Auber

♿ Few; call for appointment, tel 01 40 01 18 50

✋ Moderate

❓ Guided tours (1.5 hours) in English on Wed, Sat, Sun 11.30, 2.30; Jul–Aug daily 11.30, 2.30 (expensive, tel 0825 05 44 05)

HIGHLIGHTS

- Oscar Wilde's tomb
- Edith Piaf's tomb
- Chopin's tomb
- Marcel Proust's tomb
- Mur des Fédérés
- Delacroix's tomb
- Baron Haussmann's tomb
- Molière's tomb
- Jim Morrison's tomb

If you think cemeteries are lugubrious then a visit here may change your mind. The plethora of tomb designs, trees and twisting paths create a peaceful setting.

Pilgrimage This landscaped hillside, east of the heart of the city, is a popular haunt for rock fans, Piaf fans and lovers of poetry, literature, music and history. Since its creation in 1804 this vast cemetery has seen hundreds of the famous and illustrious buried within its precincts, so that a walk around its labyrinthine expanse presents a microcosm of French socio-cultural history. Pick up a map at the entrance or plot your visit in advance on the website.

Incumbents The cemetery was created in 1804 on Jesuit land where Louis XIV's

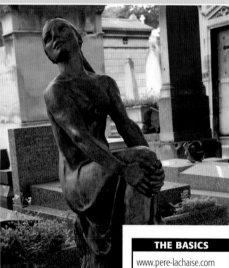

Clockwise from far left: Laid out in 1804 on the slopes of a hill in Ménilmontant, this cemetery is pleasantly shaded by trees; you can find peace and solitude at Père Lachaise; one of the many poignant statues; huge monuments and wide avenues as you wander through the cemetery

confessor, Father La Chaise, once lived. It was the site of the Communards' tragic last stand in 1871, when the 147 survivors of a night-long fight met their bloody end in front of a government firing squad and were thrown into a communal grave, now commemorated by the Mur des Fédérés in the eastern corner. Memorials also commemorate victims of the Nazi concentration camps. Paths meander past striking funerary monuments and the graves of such well-known people as the star-crossed medieval lovers Abélard and Héloïse, painters Delacroix and Modigliani, actress Sarah Bernhardt, composers Poulenc and Bizet, and writers Balzac and Colette. Crowds of rock fans throng round the tomb of Jim Morrison, singer with The Doors, who died in Paris in 1971.

THE BASICS

www.pere-lachaise.com

✚ Off map

✉ Boulevard de Ménilmontant/rue du Repos, 75020

☎ 01 55 25 82 10

🕐 Mid-Mar to early Nov Mon–Fri 8–6, Sat 8.30–6, Sun 9–6; Nov to mid-Mar Mon–Fri 8–5.30, Sat 8.30–5.30, Sun 9–5.30

🚇 Père Lachaise, Philippe Auguste, Gambetta

🚌 60, 69, 102

♿ Cobblestoned roads and hilly terrain

🎟 Free; tours moderate

❓ Guided tours (English) see www.parisinfo.com or tel 01 40 71 75 60

HIGHLIGHTS

● Jeu de Paume
● Musée de l'Orangerie
● Hôtel de Crillon (▷ 156)
● *Chevaux de Marly* (reproductions)
● View up the Champs-Élysées

As you stand in this noisy, traffic-choked square it is hard to imagine the crowds baying for the deaths of Louis XVI and Marie-Antoinette, who were both guillotined here at the height of the French Revolution.

Chop-chop This pulsating square was initially laid out in the mid-18th century to accommodate a statue of King Louis XV. Under the new name of place de la Révolution, it then witnessed the mass executions of the French Revolution and was finally renamed the place de la Concorde in 1795, as revolutionary zeal abated. In the same year Guillaume Coustou's *Chevaux de Marly* were erected at the base of the Champs-Élysées (today reproductions; the originals are in the Louvre). Crowning the

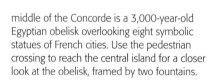

middle of the Concorde is a 3,000-year-old Egyptian obelisk overlooking eight symbolic statues of French cities. Use the pedestrian crossing to reach the central island for a closer look at the obelisk, framed by two fountains.

Grandeur To the north, on either side of the rue Royale, stand the colonnaded Hôtel de Crillon (on the left) and the matching Hôtel de la Marine (right), pre-Revolutionary relics. The rue Royale, with its luxury establishments, leads to the Madeleine. The eastern side of the Concorde is dominated by two public art galleries, both in the Jardin des Tuileries (▷ 24–25). The Jeu de Paume focuses on photography. The beautifully renovated Orangerie (nearer the river) is famous for its panels of Monet's *Water Lilies* and its Impressionist paintings.

THE BASICS

✚ E4–F4

✉ Place de la Concorde, 75008

☎ Jeu de Paume 01 47 03 12 50; www.jeude paume.org.
Musée de l'Orangerie 01 44 77 80 07; www.musee-orangerie.fr

🕐 Jeu de Paume Tue 11–9, Wed–Sun 11–7; Musée de l'Orangerie Wed–Mon 9–6

🚇 Concorde

🚌 24, 42, 52, 72, 73, 84, 94

♿ Jeu de Paume/Musée de l'Orangerie moderate

HIGHLIGHTS

- Pavillon du Roi
- Pavillon de la Reine
- Statue of Louis XIII
- No. 6, Maison de Victor Hugo
- No. 21, residence of Cardinal Richelieu
- Door knockers
- *Trompe-l'œil* bricks
- Four matching fountains

Paris's oldest and best-preserved square connects the quarters of the Marais and the Bastille. You can marvel at its architectural unity and stroll under its arcades, now animated by outdoor restaurants and window-shoppers.

Place Royale Ever since the square was inaugurated in 1612 with a spectacular fireworks display, countless luminaries have chosen to live in the redbrick houses overlooking the central garden of plane trees. Before that, the square was the site of a royal palace, the Hôtel des Tournelles (1388), which was later abandoned and demolished by Catherine de Médicis in 1559, when her husband Henri II died there. The arcaded facades were commissioned by Henri IV, who incorporated two royal

Far left: The pristine place des Vosges; left: A refreshment break in the arcade; top right: Perfect architectural symmetry; bottom right: Even the road signs are attractive

pavilions at the heart of the north and south sides of the square and named it place Royale.

Celebrities After the Revolution the square was renamed place des Vosges in tribute to the first French district to pay its new taxes. The first example of planned development in the history of Paris, these 36 town houses (nine on each side and still intact), with their steep-pitched roofs, surround a formal garden laid out with gravel paths and fountains. The symmetry of the houses has always attracted a string of celebrities, including princesses, official mistresses, Cardinal Richelieu, Victor Hugo (his house is now a museum) and Théophile Gautier. Smart shops and chic art galleries, with prices to match and ideal for window-shopping, line its arcades.

THE BASICS

www.paris.fr

➕ M6

✉ Place des Vosges, 75004

🏛 Maison Victor Hugo Tue–Sun 10–6

🍴 Several

🚇 Bastille, Chemin Vert, Saint-Paul

🚌 29, 96

♿ Good

🖐 Free

HIGHLIGHTS

● La Savoyarde bell
● View from the dome
● Mosaic of Christ
● Treasure of Sacré-Cœur
● Bronze doors at Saint-Pierre
● Stained glass
● Statue of Christ
● Statue of Virgin Mary and Child
● The funicular ride from place Saint-Pierre
● Hearing the choir sing during a service

TIP

● Sacré-Cœur is a 10-minute walk from Abbesses or Anvers Métro. Or you could take the Montmartrobus from Abbesses to place du Tertre, from where it's a short walk.

Few people would admit it, but the high point of a trip up here is not the basilica itself but the stunning views. You can't forget, however, that Sacré-Cœur was built in memory of the 58,000 dead of the Franco-Prussian War.

Weighty Although construction started in 1875, it was not until 1914 that this white neo-Romanesque-Byzantine edifice was completed, partly due to the problems of laying foundations in the quarry-riddled hill of Montmartre. Priests still work in relays to maintain the tradition of perpetual prayer for forgiveness for the horrors of war and atonement for the deaths of 58,000 people during the Franco-Prussian war of 1870–71 and the massacre of some 20,000 Communards by government

Clockwise from far left: Walking up to Sacré-Cœur; equestrian statue of Joan of Arc by Hippolyte Lefèbvre; mosaic of Christ in the basilica; one of the best views in Paris

troops. The square bell tower was an after-thought and houses one of the world's heaviest bells, La Savoyarde, which weighs in at 19 tons. The stained-glass windows are replacements of those shattered by enemy bombs in 1944.

Panoramas This unmistakable feature of the Paris skyline magnetizes the crowds arriving by funicular or via the steep steps of the terraced garden. For the best views, dawn and dusk offer particularly sparkling panoramas over the city, especially from the exterior terrace of the dome, the second-highest point in Paris after the Eiffel Tower. Just to the west of Sacré-Cœur is the diminutive Saint-Pierre, a much reworked though charming church, which is all that remains of the Benedictine abbey of Montmartre founded in 1133.

THE BASICS

www.sacre-coeur-montmartre.com

✚ c1

✉ Parvis du Sacré-Cœur, 75018

☎ 01 53 41 89 00

🕐 Daily 6am–10.30pm; dome and crypt 9.30–7 (6 in winter)

🚇 Abbesses (from here, walk along rue Yvonne Le Tac and rue Tardieu, then take funicular or walk up steps) or Anvers

🚌 Montmartrobus, 30, 31, 54, 80, 85

♿ Wheelchair access from back of basilica

💶 Basilica and crypt free; dome moderate

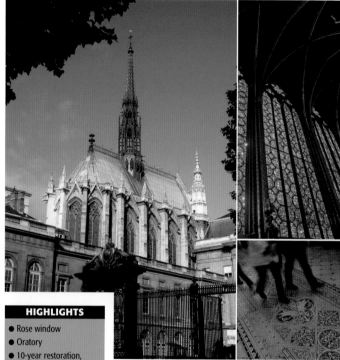

HIGHLIGHTS

● Rose window
● Oratory
● 10-year restoration, completed in 2009
● Tombs of canons
● Stained-glass depiction of Christ's Passion
● Saint Louis in the 'Story of the Relics' window

TIPS

● The upper chapel can become extremely crowded. The quietest times to visit are Tuesday and Friday morning.
● Queues for tickets can be very long; visiting La Conciergerie on a combined ticket should cut queuing.

Sainte-Chapelle's spire, soaring 75m (246ft) above the ground, is in itself a great expression of faith, but this is surpassed, inside, by the glowing intensity of the stained-glass windows reaching up to a star-studded roof, now spectacularly restored.

Masterpiece One of Paris's oldest and most significant monuments stands in the precincts of the Palais de Justice. The chapel was built by Louis IX (later canonized) to house relics he had acquired at exorbitant cost during the crusades, and which included what was reputed to be the Crown of Thorns, as well as fragments of the Cross and drops of Christ's blood (now kept in Notre-Dame). Pierre de Montreuil is believed to have masterminded this delicate Gothic construction, bypassing the use of flying buttresses,

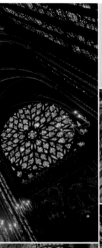

Clockwise from far left: Sainte-Chapelle, with fine buttresses and a delicate spire; superb stained glass, depicting biblical scenes and featuring a rose window; intricate wood carving in the upper chapel; looking up at the magnificent ceiling; colourful wood carving; ornate patterned flooring

incorporating a lower chapel for palace servants to worship in and installing more than 600sq m (6,458sq ft) of striking stained glass above. Completed in 1248 in record time, it was Louis IX's private chapel, with discreet access from what was then the royal palace.

Apocalypse More than 1,000 biblical scenes are illustrated in 15 windows, starting with Genesis in the window to the left of the entrance, and working round the chapel to finish with the Apocalypse, in the rose window. The only non-biblical theme is in the 16th window, which tells how the holy relics came to Paris. Two-thirds of the windows are 13th-century originals—the oldest stained glass in Paris. The statues of the Apostles are copies; the damaged originals are at the Musée National du Moyen-Âge (▷ 34–35).

THE BASICS

www.sainte-chapelle.
monuments-nationaux.fr

🔛 J6

✉ 4 boulevard du Palais, Île de la Cité, 75001

☎ 01 53 40 60 80

🕐 Mar–Oct 9.30–6; Nov–Feb daily 9–5

Ⓜ Cité, Châtelet

🚌 21, 27, 38, 85, 96

🚉 RER Line B, St-Michel

♿ Moderate (joint ticket with the Conciergerie expensive)

❓ Guided tours in English by appointment only; tel 01 53 40 60 93

THE BOAT TRIP

Distance: 11km (7 miles)
Allow: Just over 1 hour
Start/End: Square du Vert-Galant, Pont Neuf
How to get there:
🚇 Pont Neuf
🚌 24, 27, 58, 67, 70, 72, 74, 75
From the Métro station, walk over the Pont Neuf. About halfway across, on the right, is a sign for the Vedettes du Pont Neuf. Go down the steps to the square.

TIPS

● Evening is a great time to go on this trip, when the monuments are lit up.
● A more flexible—though no cheaper—way to enjoy the river is the hop-on, hop-off Batobus shuttle service (▷ 167).

A pleasant river cruise along the Seine is a great way to view some of Paris's key sights from a different perspective. And in just over an hour you can see many of the famous landmarks.

Romantic trip The boat leaves from square du Vert-Galant and heads west. On the Right Bank you can see the Museé du Louvre (▷ 30–31). After passing under the Pont du Carrousel and the Pont Royal you'll see the Musée d'Orsay (▷ 36–37) on the Left Bank and then the 18th-century Palais Bourbon. On the Right Bank is place de la Concorde (▷ 50–51). The boat passes under the ornate Pont Alexandre III (▷ 73). On the Right Bank is the Grand Palais and Petit Palais and on the Left Bank, in the distance, is Les Invalides (▷ 68–69). After

Clockwise from far left: View of Notre-Dame across the river; boats ply past the Eiffel Tower; a bateau-mouche trip along the Seine; boats at the Pont Neuf; a fine view of the Eiffel Tower and the footbridge, the Passerelle Debilly

passing under the Pont des Invalides, the Pont de l'Alma and the Passerelle Debilly, the boat rounds a bend to unveil a spectacular view of the Eiffel Tower (▷ 60–61) on the Left Bank. The boat passes under the Pont d'Iéna, which spans the river between the Eiffel Tower and the Jardins du Trocadéro, before turning and heading back in the opposite direction to the Île de la Cité. You'll see the cupola of the Institut de France on the right before you pass under the southern side of the Pont Neuf. The next two bridges are the Pont Saint-Michel, leading to the Latin Quarter and the Sorbonne university, and the Petit Pont, the smallest bridge in Paris. On the Île de la Cité you can see Notre-Dame cathedral (▷ 44–45); the boat then circles the picturesque Île St. Louis before returning to the Pont Neuf past the Conciergerie.

THE BASICS

www.vedettesdupontneuf.com

☎ 01 46 33 98 38

🕐 Mid-Mar to Oct daily 10.30, 11.15, 12, then every half-hour from 1.30 to 7, then 8, 9, 9.30, 10, 10.30; Nov to mid- Mar Mon–Thu 10.30, 11.15, 12, 2, 2.45, 3.30, 4.15, 5, 5.45, 6.30, 8 and 10, Fri–Sun 10.30, 11.15, 12, 2, 2.45, 3.30, 4.15, 5, 5.45, 6.30, 8, 9, 10. Times may vary

💰 Expensive

❓ Pick up a free route map from the boarding platform

HIGHLIGHTS

- Panoramic views
- Gustave Eiffel's office
- Sparkling lights

TIPS

- To skip the wait for the elevators, walk up the stairs to level two, then catch the elevator to the top. The climb isn't too daunting. Alternatively buy your tickets online.
- The wait for the elevator is generally shorter at night.
- Pushchairs (strollers) are allowed up the tower only if they are collapsible.

The Eiffel Tower could be a cliché but it isn't. The powerful silhouette of Gustave Eiffel's marvel of engineering still makes a stirring sight, especially at night when its delicate, lace-like iron structure comes to the fore.

Glittering feat Built in a record two years for the 1889 Exposition Universelle, the Eiffel Tower was never intended to be a permanent feature of the city. However, in 1910 it was finally saved for posterity, preparing the way for today's 6.7 million annual visitors. Avoid a long wait for the elevator by visiting the tower at night, when it fully lives up to its romantic image and provides a glittering spectacle whether from the illumination of the tower itself or the carpet of nocturnal Paris unfolding at its

Clockwise from far left: The icon of Paris set in the Champ de Mars; view of the tower from the Jardins du Trocadéro; the tower framed by the Wall of Peace; detail of the lace-like iron structure; the lower section dwarfs the crowds

feet. More than 330 spotlights illuminate the latticework, topped by a rotating beacon. After dusk the tower sparkles for 5 minutes every hour on the hour until 1am, thanks to 20,000 randomly flashing low-energy bulbs.

Violent reactions Gustave Eiffel was a master of cast-iron structures; his prolific output included hundreds of factories, churches, via-ducts and bridges on four continents. His 324m (1,063ft) tower attracted great opposition, but his genius was vindicated by the fact that it sways no more than 9cm (3.5in) in high winds and it remained the world's highest structure for 40 years. Eiffel kept an office here until his death in 1923; at the top, there is a re-creation of Thomas Edison's visit to Eiffel on 10 September 1889.

THE BASICS

www.tour-eiffel.fr

➕ B6

✉ Quai Branly, Champ de Mars, 75007

☎ 01 44 11 23 23

🕐 Sep to mid-Jun daily 9.30am–11.45pm (stairs 9.30–6.30); mid-Jun to Aug 9am–12.45am; last lift at 11pm

🍴 Le 58 (1st floor, 01 45 55 20 04); Le Jules Verne (2nd floor, ▷ 149)

🚇 Bir-Hakeim, Trocadéro

🚌 42, 69, 82, 87

🚊 RER Line C, Tour Eiffel

♿ Very good (to 2nd floor). Wheelchair users unable to go to very top

💰 Expensive; stairs moderate

HIGHLIGHTS

- Hall of Mirrors
- Petit Trianon
- Formal gardens
- Grandes Eaux
- Hameau and farm
- Buffet d'Eau, Grand Trianon
- Opera house

TIP

- Attend a performance to see the interior of the splendid 18th-century royal opera house.

The Château de Versailles has undergone a massive renovation that has restored much of the grandeur enjoyed by the Sun King, Louis XIV.

A new palace Versailles is the ultimate symbol of French grandeur, and the backdrop to the death of the monarchy in 1789. Louis XIV moved his court to the site of his father's hunting lodge, creating a royal residence, seat of government and home to French nobility. Building continued until his death in 1715, by which time the 100ha (247-acre) garden had been perfected by landscape garden designer André Le Nôtre.

Glorious gardens With their geometric beds, vast watercourses and splendid fountains

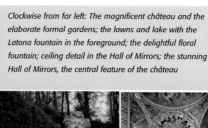

Clockwise from far left: The magnificent château and the elaborate formal gardens; the lawns and lake with the Latona fountain in the foreground; the delightful floral fountain; ceiling detail in the Hall of Mirrors; the stunning Hall of Mirrors, the central feature of the château

(flowing weekends Apr–Oct) the palace gardens are the perfect expression of the formal French style. Geometry rules, too, in the floral gardens at the lavish royal retreat of Grand Trianon, but Marie-Antoinette's romantic estate at Petit Trianon is informal and pretty. It comprises a small château, belvedere, hamlet (Hameau de la Reine) and the notorious but delightful farm where she liked to play at being a milkmaid.

Architectural highlights The bellicose magnificence of the Hall of Mirrors is the highlight of the Grands Appartements, where you can also see the opulent Queen's Chamber, restored now to how it looked when Marie Antoinette fled the mob here in 1789. At weekends, you can visit the more intimate apartments of the Dauphin and Louis XV's daughters.

THE BASICS

www.chateauversailles.fr

➕ Off map

✉ Place d'Armes, Versailles

☎ 01 30 83 78 00

🕐 State apartments Apr–Oct Tue–Sun 9–6.30; Nov–Mar Tue–Sun 9–5.30. Grand and Petit Trianon Tue–Sun 12–5.30 (until 6.30 in summer). Park daily 7am–8.30pm (8–6 in winter). Fountains Apr–Oct Sat–Sun 11–12, 3.30–5.30

🚉 RER C, Versailles Rive Gauche

♿ Few (State apartments)

✋ Passport ticket for all palaces expensive (visitors with disabilities free); park free; Grandes Eaux and Jardins Musicaux moderate Apr–Oct. (If you already have tickets, go to the A access. If not, go to the Ticket Information point, South Ministers' Wing.) Free first Sun of month Nov–Mar

❓ Guided tour

More to See

This section contains other great places to visit if you have more time. Some are in the heart of the city while others are a short journey away, found under Further Afield. This chapter also has fantastic excursions that you should set aside a whole day to visit.

MORE TO SEE

BIBLIOTHÈQUE NATIONALE DE FRANCE–FRANÇOIS MITTERRAND

www.bnf.fr

Around 13 million books and documents are owned by the BNF. The modern library, with its glass corner towers designed like four open books, is on the east edge of the Left Bank.

➕ Off map at M9 ✉ Quai François-Mauriac, 75013 ☎ 01 53 79 59 59 🕐 Upper Garden reading rooms Mon 2–7, Tue–Sat 9–7, Sun 1–7 🚇 Bibliothèque François-Mitterrand

CAFÉ BEAUBOURG

Opposite the Pompidou Centre, this café is liked by artists, critics and book-reading poseurs. Discreet tables in a big room are designed by Christian de Portzamparc.

➕ K5 ✉ 43 rue Saint-Merri, 75004 ☎ 01 48 87 63 96 🕐 Daily 8am–midnight 🚇 Hôtel de Ville, Châtelet, Rambuteau

CAFÉ LES DEUX MAGOTS

www.lesdeuxmagots.fr

This famous Left Bank café has a good mix of tourists and the literary shades of Albert Camus and Hemingway.

➕ G7 ✉ 170 boulevard Saint-Germain/6 place Saint-Germain-des-Prés, 75006 ☎ 01 45 48 55 25 🕐 Daily 7.30am–1am 🚇 Saint-Germain-des-Prés

CAFÉ DE FLORE

www.cafedeflore.fr

Haunted by ghosts of existentialists Sartre and de Beauvoir, who held court here during the Occupation, this café is pricey but a good spot for people-watching over a cup of hot chocolate.

➕ G7 ✉ 172 boulevard Saint-Germain, 75006 ☎ 01 45 48 55 26 🕐 Daily 7am–2am 🚇 Saint-Germain-des-Prés

CIMETIÈRE DE MONTMARTRE

Montmartre's cemetery is packed with graves of the famous, including composers Hector Berlioz and Jacques Offenbach, writers Henri Stendhal and Alexandre Dumas, artists Edgar Degas and Jean-Baptiste Greuze, film-maker François Truffaut and singer Dalida. The imposing tomb of Émile Zola is close to the flower-filled

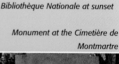

Bibliothèque Nationale at sunset

Monument at the Cimetière de Montmartre

roundabout near the main entrance, although the writer's remains were moved to the Panthéon in 1908.

🚇 a1 ✉ 20 avenue Rachel, 75018 ☎ 01 53 42 36 30 🕐 Mid-Mar to early Nov Mon–Fri 8–6, Sat 8.30–6, Sun 9–6; Nov to mid-Mar Mon–Fri 8–5.30, Sat 8.30–5.30, Sun 9–5.30 (last entry 15 min before closing) 🚇 Place de Clichy, Blanche

DROUOT RICHELIEU

www.drouot.com

Paris's main auction rooms are where anything from a Persian carpet or a Louis XV commode may come under the hammer.

🚇 H2 ✉ 9 rue Drouot, 75009 ☎ 01 48 00 20 20 🕐 Mon–Sat 11–6 (most auctions start at 2pm); closed Aug 🚇 Richelieu-Drouot

ÉGLISE SAINT-ÉTIENNE-DU-MONT

Dating from the 15th century, this church has a bizarre combination of Gothic, Renaissance and classical architecture. The unique screen arching over the nave is a highlight, with its delicate fretwork.

🚇 J8 ✉ Place Sainte-Geneviève, 75005 🕐 Tue–Fri 8.45–7.30, Sat 8.45–12, 2–7.45, Sun 8.45–12.15, 2–7.45 (hours can vary during holidays) 🚇 Cardinal Lemoine

ÉGLISE SAINT-EUSTACHE

www.saint-eustache.org

Renaissance in detail and decoration but Gothic in general design, this church has frequent concerts.

🚇 J4 ✉ 2 impasse Saint-Eustache, 75001 🕐 Mon–Fri 9.30–7, Sat–Sun 9–7 🚇 Les Halles

ÉGLISE SAINT-GERMAIN-DES-PRÉS

Paris's oldest church dates from the 11th century and preserves its 12th-century flying buttresses, an original tower and the choir. There are organ and concert recitals.

🚇 G6 ✉ Place Saint-Germain-des-Prés, 75006 🕐 Daily 9–7 🚇 Saint-Germain-des-Prés

ÉGLISE SAINT-MERRI

A superb example of Flamboyant Gothic, not completed until 1612. You'll find Renaissance stained glass, murals, an impressive organ

Église Saint-Eustache

Église Saint-Germain-des-Prés

loft and Paris's oldest church bell (1331). It also holds concerts.
🔳 K5 ✉ 76 rue de la Verrerie, 75004 ☎ www.accueilmusical.fr for concert information 🚇 Hôtel de Ville

ÉGLISE SAINT-SÉVERIN
www.saint-severin.com
Built from the 13th to 16th centuries on the site of an 11th-century church, the interior features lovely stained glass and palm-tree vaulting.
🔳 J7 ✉ 3 rue des Prêtres Saint-Séverin, 75005 🕐 Mon–Sat 11–7.30, Sun 9–8.30 🚇 Saint-Michel, Cluny La Sorbonne

ÉGLISE SAINT-SULPICE
www.paroisse-saint-sulpice-paris.org
Work started here in 1646, ending 134 years later with asymmetrical towers and mixed styles. Note Delacroix's murals in the first chapel on the right and 18th-century wood panelling in the sacristy.
🔳 G7 ✉ Place Saint-Sulpice, 75006 🕐 Daily 7.30–7.30 🚇 Saint-Sulpice

ÎLE SAINT-LOUIS
The Île Saint-Louis maintains a spirit of its own; an oasis of calm.

Rue Saint-Louis-en-l'Île is lined with art shops and restaurants.
🔳 K/L7 🚇 Pont Marie, Sully Morland

INSTITUT DU MONDE ARABE
www.imarabe.org
The high tech reinterpretation of traditional Arab fretwork is the hallmark here. The museum has fine metalwork, ceramics, textiles, carpets and calligraphy.
🔳 K7 ✉ 1 rue des Fossés Saint-Bernard, 75005 ☎ 01 40 51 38 38 🕐 Tue–Fri 10–6, Sat–Sun 10–7. Library Tue–Sat 1–8 🚇 Cardinal Lemoine, Jussieu

LES INVALIDES
www.invalides.org
Les Invalides was built to house invalid soldiers and continues to accommodate a few today. The greatest figures of French military history, most notably Napoleon himself, are interred in the Église du Dôme, while their battles and campaigns are illustrated in the Musée de l'Armée.
🔳 D6 ✉ 129 rue de Grenelle, 75007 🕐 Apr–Oct daily 10–6 (Tue until 9); Nov–Mar 10–5. Closed first Mon of month

Vaulted ceiling, Gothic arches and stained glass inside Église Saint-Séverin

(except Jul–Sep). Église du Dôme until 9pm Apr–Sep 🚇 La Tour Maubourg, École Militaire, Varenne 🎫 Moderate

JARDIN DU PALAIS ROYAL

Elegant 18th-century shopping arcades surround this peaceful garden and palace (now the Conseil Constitutionnel and the Ministère de la Culture). Daniel Buren's striking striped columns occupy the Cour d'Honneur.

➕ H4 ✉ Place du Palais-Royal, 75001 🕐 Apr–May daily 7am–10.15pm; Jun–Aug 7am–11pm; Sep 7am–9.30pm; Oct–Mar 7.30am–8.30pm 🍴 Plenty 🚇 Palais-Royal–Musée du Louvre

MAISON EUROPÉENNE DE LA PHOTOGRAPHIE

www.mep-fr.org

This is a stylish complex for contemporary photography, with dynamic temporary shows. The galleries are spread over five floors of the 18th-century Hôtel Hénault de Cantobre, and a new wing.

➕ L6 ✉ 5–7 rue de Fourcy, 75004 ☎ 01 44 78 75 00 🕐 Wed–Sun 11am–8pm 🚇 Saint-Paul 🎫 Moderate

MÉMORIAL DE LA SHOAH

www.memorialdelashoah.org

This moving and impressive Holocaust museum contains a wall inscribed with the names of the 76,000 Jewish people deported from France between 1942 and 1944. In addition to its permanent displays it also mounts temporary exhibitions on Holocaust-related themes.

➕ K6 ✉ 17 rue Geoffroy-l'Asnier, 75004 ☎ 01 42 77 44 72 🕐 Sun–Fri 10–6 (Thu until 10) 🚇 Saint-Paul, Hôtel de Ville, Pont Marie

MUSÉE D'ART ET D'HISTOIRE DU JUDAÏSME

www.mahj.org

Jewish art and culture are on display here, from medieval times to the present day, concentrating mainly on France but also including the rest of Europe and North Africa. Exhibits range from wedding items, *objets d'art*, manuscripts and textiles to works by Jewish artists such as Modigliani and Chagall.

➕ K5 ✉ Hôtel de Saint-Aignan, 71 rue du Temple, 75003 ☎ 01 53 01 86 60

MORE TO SEE

Sign at Maison Européenne de la Photographie

The formal gardens in front of Les Invalides

🕐 Mon–Fri 11–6, Sun 10–6
🚇 Rambuteau, Hôtel de Ville 💶 Moderate

MUSÉE D'ART MODERNE DE LA VILLE DE PARIS

www.mam.paris.fr

Outstanding temporary exhibitions help keep this modern-art museum within an international sphere. The collection covers Fauvism, Cubism, Surrealism, Abstraction and Nouveau Réalisme. *La Danse* (1932), a mural by Henri Matisse, hangs in a room devoted to the artist. The museum occupies the east wing of the Palais de Tokyo; the west wing houses the Centre d'Art Contemporain.

➕ B4 ✉ 11 avenue du Président Wilson, 75016 ☎ 01 53 67 40 00 🕐 Tue–Wed 10–6, Thu 10–10, Fri–Sun 10–6 🚇 Iéna, Alma-Marceau 💶 Free. Temporary exhibitions: moderate

MUSÉE DES ARTS DÉCORATIFS

www.lesartsdecoratifs.fr

A magnificent collection of decorative arts are displayed in this beautifully restored space.

Throughout the 20th century contributions by designers such as Le Corbusier, Mallet-Stevens, Niki de Saint Phalle and Philippe Starck greatly enriched the collections.

➕ G5 ✉ 107 rue de Rivoli, 75001 ☎ 01 44 55 57 50 🕐 Tue–Sun 11–6 (Thu until 9) 🚇 Palais-Royal–Musée du Louvre 💶 Moderate

MUSÉE DES ARTS ET MÉTIERS

www.arts-et-metiers.net

Art meets science at this fascinating museum through antique clocks, optics, underwater items including a diving suit, vintage cars and mechanical toys.

➕ K4 ✉ 60 rue Réaumur, 75003 ☎ 01 53 01 82 00 🕐 Tue–Sun 10–6 (Thu until 9.30pm) 🚇 Arts et Métiers, Réaumur-Sébastopol 💶 Moderate

MUSÉE COGNACQ-JAY

www.cognacq-jay.paris.fr

In a mansion furnished in 18th-century style, you can see the 18th-century paintings and *objets d'art* collected by Ernest Cognacq and his wife Louise Jay, founders of the La Samaritaine store.

Musée d'Art Moderne de la Ville de Paris

Modern design at the Musée des Arts Décoratifs

L6 ✉ Hôtel Donon, 8 rue Elzévir, 75003
☎ 01 40 27 07 21 🕐 Tue–Sun 10–6
Ⓜ Saint-Paul 🎫 Free

MUSÉE GUSTAVE MOREAU

www.musee-moreau.fr

This studio-museum, on the edge of Pigalle, offers an intriguing view of how a late-19th-century artist lived. On the second and third floors are the studios of the symbolist painter Gustave Moreau (1826–98), teacher to Henri Matisse. On the first floor is a reconstruction of his private apartment. The museum is closed for renovation from July 15 until December 2013.

G2 ✉ 14 rue de la Rochefoucauld, 75009 ☎ 01 48 74 38 50 🕐 Wed–Mon 10–12.45, 2–5.15 🎫 Moderate; free first Sun of month Ⓜ Trinité

MUSÉE JACQUEMART-ANDRÉ

www.musee-jacquemart-andre.com

An elegant mansion hosts this fine collection of around 150 paintings, including works by Botticelli, Rembrandt, Bellini, Van Dyck, Fragonard and David.

D2 ✉ 158 boulevard Haussmann, 75008 ☎ 01 45 62 11 59 🕐 Daily 10–6
Ⓜ Saint-Philippe-du-Roule, Miromesnil 🎫 Moderate (audioguide included)

MUSÉE DE MONTMARTRE

www.museedemontmartre.fr

Montmartre's history is arguably the most enchanting of all Paris's districts, with its walking beheaded saint, prosperous windmills and infamous nightlife. You can find out more at the unassuming Musée de Montmartre.

c1 ✉ 12 rue Cortot, 75018 ☎ 01 49 25 89 37 🕐 Daily 10–6 Ⓜ Lamarck Caulaincourt, Anvers 🎫 Moderate

MUSÉUM NATIONAL D'HISTOIRE NATURELLE, JARDIN DES PLANTES

www.mnhn.fr

Set up in 1635 on the initiative of Louis XIII's physician, the magnificent Jardin des Plantes is Paris's botanical garden, complete with an alpine garden and hothouses. Ranged around its fringes are the buildings of the Muséum National d'Histoire Naturelle, of which the

Paintings at the Musée Gustave Moreau

Facade of the Musée Gustave Moreau

garden itself forms part. These include the Galeries de Paléontologie with its dinosaur skeletons and the Grande Galerie de l'Évolution, which has a children's gallery devoted to biodiversity.

➕ K9–L8/9 ✉ 57 rue Cuvier, 75005 ☎ 01 40 79 54 79 🕐 Jardin daily 7.30–7 (Apr–Sep until 8); Grande Galerie Wed–Mon 10–6. Galeries de Paléontologie Wed–Mon 10–5 🚇 Place Monge, Jussieu 💰 Jardin free, others moderate

PALAIS DE CHAILLOT

Built for the Paris exhibition of 1937, the majestic curving wings of the Palais de Chaillot house the Musée de la Marine, the Musée de l'Homme (reopening in 2015), the Cité de l'Architecture et du Patrimoine and Théâtre de Chaillot. The wide terraced Parvis des Libertés et des Droits de l'Homme, between the two wings, offers breathtaking views across the city.

➕ A5 ✉ Place du Trocadéro, 75116 ☎ Marine: 01 53 65 69 69; www.musee-marine.fr. Homme: 01 44 05 72 87; www.museedelhomme.fr 🚇 Trocadéro 💰 Moderate

PANTHÉON

www.monuments-nationaux.fr

Occupying a hilltop site close to the Sorbonne and the Quartier Latin, Soufflot's cathedral-like neo-classical 18th-century structure provides an imposing setting for the tombs of France's greatest citizens, including Voltaire, Dumas, Rousseau and Marie Curie. From April to October, you can ascend the dome as part of a guided tour.

➕ J8 ✉ Place du Panthéon, 75005 ☎ 01 44 32 18 00 🕐 Apr–Sep daily 10–6.30; Oct–Mar 10–6 🚇 Cardinal Lemoine, Maubert Mutualité 💰 Moderate

PARC DU CHAMP DE MARS

The lawns of the Champ de Mars stretch out in a rectangular design between the Eiffel Tower and the 18th-century École Militaire. The Romans fought the Celtic Parisii tribe here in 52bc—the park's name, Field of Mars, refers to the Roman god of war. It wasn't until 1765 that the site became a parade ground for the École Militaire's young cadets. The park has hosted national celebrations, parades,

Aerial view of the Champ de Mars from the Eiffel Tower

international exhibitions, horse races and early hot-air ballooning experiments. Today it is popular with families, joggers and visitors.

➕ B6–C6 ✉ Champ de Mars, 75007
🚇 École Militaire

PARC DE MONCEAU

This classic park, redesigned in 1793 by Thomas Blaikie, is full of follies and picturesque faux ruins.

➕ D1 ✉ 35 boulevard de Courcelles, 75008 🕐 May–Aug daily 7am–10pm; Sep 7am–9pm; Oct–Apr 7am–8pm
🚇 Monceau 🎟 Free

PAVILLON DE L'ARSENAL

www.pavillon-arsenal.com

This strikingly designed building houses well-conceived exhibitions on urban Paris past and present, alongside a display on the city's architectural evolution.

➕ L7 ✉ 21 boulevard Morland, 75004
☎ 01 42 76 33 97 🕐 Tue–Sat 10.30–6.30, Sun 11–7 🚇 Sully Morland 🎟 Free

PLACE DES ABBESSES

Place des Abbesses is less touristy than place du Tertre, farther up the Montmartre hill, so it's a quieter coffee stop. The magnificent art nouveau Métro entrance here leads into Paris's deepest station, 30m (98.5ft) below ground. It was designed by Hector Guimard (1867–1942) and is one of only three original Guimard entrances left in Paris. The church of Saint-Jean-de-Montmartre (1904) picks up on the art nouveau theme, with decorative windows that enliven the rather ugly redbrick cladding.

➕ c2 ✉ Place des Abbesses, Montmartre, 75018 🚇 Abbesses

PONT ALEXANDRE III

Four gilded bronze Pegasus figures watch over this wildly ornate bridge, which forms a link between Les Invalides (▷ 68–69) on the Left Bank and the Grand Palais and Petit Palais on the Right. Symbolic of the optimism of the Belle Époque, it was built for the 1900 Exposition Universelle. The bridge is crammed with elaborate decoration by more than 15 artists.

➕ D4 ✉ Cours de la Reine/quai d'Orsay
🚇 Invalides, Champs-Élysées–Clémenceau

Art nouveau entrance to the Abbesses Métro station, designed by Hector Guimard

Bronze figures on the Pont Alexandre III

PONT DE L'ALMA

The first Pont de l'Alma was built in 1856 to commemorate a victory over the Russians by the Franco-British alliance in the Crimean War. The bridge was replaced in 1974. The underpass on the Right Bank is where the fatal car crash involving Diana, Princess of Wales, occurred in August 1997. The Liberty Flame near the entrance, a symbol of American and French friendship, has become an unofficial memorial.

✚ C4/C5 ✉ Place de l'Alma/place de la Résistance 🚇 Alma-Marceau

PONT DES ARTS

The pedestrian bridge of 1804 was replaced in 1984 by a new iron structure of seven steel arches crossed by resonant wooden planks. It's a popular spot for impromptu parties and lively street performances.

✚ H5–6 🚇 Louvre-Rivoli

PONT DE BIR-HAKEIM

The bridge was built between 1903 and 1905. The two-tier art nouveau structure has a walkway, roadway and a Métro viaduct. It is made up of two unequal metal structures on either side of the allée des Cygnes. The bridge was given its name in 1949, in memory of the victory of General Koenig in Libya in 1942.

✚ A6 ✉ Quai Branly/avenue du Président Kennedy 🚇 Bir-Hakeim, Passy

PONT NEUF

Dating from 1604, Paris's oldest bridge ironically bears the name of 'New Bridge'. The houseless design was highly controversial at the time.

✚ H6 🚇 Pont Neuf, Île de la Cité

RUE DU CHERCHE-MIDI

César's sculpture on the rue de Sèvres crossroads marks out this typical Left Bank street, home to the famous Poîlane bakery (No. 8) and the Musée Hébert (No. 85).

✚ G7 🚇 Saint-Sulpice

RUE DU FAUBOURG SAINT-HONORÉ

Price tags and politics cohabit in this street of luxury. Admire

Pont de Bir-Hakeim

Houses behind the Pont Neuf

Hermès' imaginative window dressing or salute the gendarmes in front of the Élysée Palace.

⊞ E3 🚇 Madeleine, Miromesnil

RUE JACOB

Antiques and interior-decoration shops monopolize this picturesque stretch. Make a 20-pace detour to the Musée Delacroix on the rue de Furstenberg.

⊞ G6 🚇 Saint-Germain-des-Prés

RUE DES ROSIERS

An effervescent street set at the heart of Paris's Jewish quarter, with synagogues, kosher butchers and restaurants, Hebrew bookshops and designer boutiques.

⊞ L6 🚇 Saint-Paul

RUE VIEILLE-DU-TEMPLE

The pulse of the hip Marais district, this street is dense with bars, cafés, restaurants and boutiques.

⊞ K6–L5 🚇 Saint-Paul

SQUARE DU VERT-GALANT

Enjoy a quintessential view of bridges and the Louvre in this tiny, pretty park, perfect for a picnic.

⊞ H6 ✉ Place du Pont-Neuf, 75001 🕐 May–Aug daily 9–9; Apr, Sep 9–8; Oct–Mar 9–6.30 🚇 Pont Neuf

TOUR MONTPARNASSE

www.tourmontparnasse56.com

When it was constructed in 1973, with its reinforced concrete core, the Tour Montparnasse's 59 floors of smoked glass provoked not a little indignation. Since then it has become a familiar landmark, visible from all over Paris, and is spectacular by night when the many hundreds of windows light up the sky. The 56th-floor viewing gallery and the 59th-floor terrace of this 209m (685ft) tower offer breathtaking views of the city. On a clear day you can see up to 40km (25 miles) away. Films on Paris (in French) are screened on the 56th floor.

⊞ F9 ✉ 33 avenue du Maine, 75015 ☎ 01 45 38 52 56 🕐 Apr–Sep daily 9.30am–11.30pm; Oct–Mar 9.30am–10.30pm (until 11 Fri–Sat). Last elevator up is 30 min before closing 🚇 Montparnasse-Bienvenüe 💷 Moderate

Buildings reflected in a Lanvin shop window at 15 rue du Faubourg Saint-Honoré

Square du Vert-Galant

Further Afield

LA GRANDE ARCHE

www.grandearche.com

A modernist white marble echo of the Arc de Triomphe on a giant scale designed by Johann Otto von Spreckelsen for the 1989 Bicentennial. On the roof-top is a Computer Museum.

🗷 Off map 🖂 1 parvis de La Défense ☎ 01 49 07 27 55 🕑 Daily 10–8 (7 in winter) 🚇 Grande Arche de La Défense

PARC ANDRÉ-CITROËN

A futurist 1990s park divided into specialist gardens, on the site of a former Citroën factory. You'll find zany experimentation with metal and water, plus a tethered balloon.

🗷 Off map 🖂 Rue Cauchy, 75015 🕑 Daily 9–dusk 🚇 Balard, Javel 🎟 Free

PARC DES BUTTES CHAUMONT

The loveliest of Haussmann's parks owes its singular beauty and fine views to its craggy site, a former quarry in the northeast of the city. There is also a children's puppet theatre, the Guignol de Paris.

🗷 Off map 🖂 1 rue Botzaris, 75019 🕑 May–Aug daily 7am–10pm; Sep 7am–9pm; Oct–Apr 7am–8pm 🚇 Buttes Chaumont 🎟 Free

PARC DE LA VILLETTE

www.villette.com

The ultramodern Parc de la Villette, built on the former site of the city's abbatoirs, catapults you into a futuristic world with a range of cultural and leisure activities. There's a science museum, music complex, hemispheric cinema, exhibition venue and concert hall. A covered walkway runs the length of the park, linking the Cité de Sciences et de l'Industrie and Cité de la Musique. At the Musée de la Musique nearly 1,000 musical instruments are showcased.

🗷 Off map 🖂 Park: 211 avenue Jean-Jaurès; Cité des Sciences: 30 avenue Corentin-Cariou, 75019 ☎ Park: 01 40 03 75 75; Cité des Sciences: 01 40 05 70 00 🕑 Cité des Sciences: Tue–Sat 10–6, Sun 10–7. Cité de la Musique: Tue–Sat 12–6, Sun 10–6 🍽 Cafés, restaurants 🚇 Park: Porte de Pantin; Cité des Sciences: Porte de la Villette 🎟 Park: free; Cité des Sciences: expensive 🛈 Reserve shows, films and activities as soon as you arrive

La Grande Arche in the La Défense business district

Excursions

CHANTILLY

www.chateaudechantilly.com

The Château de Chantilly is one of the most picturesque castles in the region. It is surrounded by attractive parkland, with the forest of Chantilly beyond, and contains a magnificent art collection. The town of Chantilly is one of the leading training venues in Europe for racehorses and is home to a world-famous racecourse and the Musée Vivant du Cheval horse museum, which is housed in the Grandes Écuries—a magnificent 18th-century stable block.

For five centuries, the domain of Chantilly passed from one branch of the same family to another without ever being sold, starting with the Orgemont family in the 14th and 15th centuries before passing to the Montmorencys, one of the most powerful families in the kingdom. Chantilly passed in turn to the Bourbon Condés, cousins of the kings of France.

The old château was ruined during the Revolution, but in the late 19th century a splendid reconstruction was commissioned by Henri d'Orléans, duc d'Aumale, the son of King Louis Philippe, who needed somewhere to house his art collection. It is still hung in the Galerie des Peintures in the manner stipulated by him when he bequeathed Chantilly to the nation. The collection includes works by Raphael and Botticelli, Watteau, Delacroix and Ingres. The château opened as a museum in 1898, a year after the duke's death. The Grands Appartements are in the Renaissance wing of the Petit Château adjacent to the main building, and include the charming Grande Singerie, an 18th-century boudoir decorated with images of monkeys and chinoiserie.

Distance: 48km (30 miles)

Journey Time: 24 min (SNCF train)/45 min (RER train)

🔲 Off map ☎ 03 44 27 31 80

🔘 Château Apr–Sep daily 10–6; Oct Wed–Mon 10.30–6; Nov–Dec Wed–Mon 10.30–5. Grand Stables and Musée Vivant same as Château 🚉 Chantilly-Gouvieux SNCF, RER line D; free bus from station to château

🎟 Château expensive

The delightful Château de Chantilly

A winged statue in the Temple of Love, in the grounds of Château de Chantilly

DISNEYLAND RESORT PARIS

www.disneylandparis.com

Disneyland Resort Paris attracts millions of visitors to its two Parks—Disneyland Park and Walt Disney Studios Park. The resort, in the Marne-la-Vallée countryside east of Paris, opened in 1992. The Walt Disney Studios Park was added in 2002. Other attractions include the Disney Village entertainment complex, eight hotels and even a golf course.

Disneyland Paris offers the traditional Disney experience with family-friendly attractions such as Main Street USA, with its recreation of small town America in the first part of the 20th century, an old-fashioned steam train and horse-drawn streetcars. There are rides to suit all ages and levels of bravery, from the charming musical journey of It's a Small World, the lavish Pirates of the Caribbean ride and Buzz Lightyear Laser Blast—a laser shoot-out—to the white-knuckle rides such as Space Mountain: Mission 2 and Big Thunder Mountain, in which you take a journey on a runaway mine train. Minimum height and age restrictions apply on some rides. Walt Disney Studios Park's scarier rides include the terrifying Tower of Terror—an abandoned art deco hotel in which the elevator drops at faster than the speed of gravity —and the Rock n' Roller Coaster, a fast, looping roller coaster that propels you from 0 to 100kph (62mph) in just three seconds.

Much of what there is to see in Walt Disney Studios Park is specifically film-related and includes the spectacular stunt driving of Moteurs...Action! and the animation-themed attractions of Toon Studio. At Art of Disney Animation you'll learn the techniques used to animate a Disney cartoon before getting the opportunity to try it for yourself. You can also take the Studio Tram Tour through the special effects of Catastrophe Canyon.

Distance: 44km (27 miles)

Journey Time: 35 min

🚇 Off map ✉ Marne-la-Vallée, 77777, Cedex 4 ☎ 0825 300 222 🚆 RER Line A, Marne-la-Vallée 🎫 Expensive

Sleeping Beauty's Castle, Disneyland Resort Paris
Space Mountain, Disneyland Resort Paris

FONTAINEBLEAU

www.musee-chateau-fontainebleau.fr

Fontainebleau has witnessed momentous events, including the birth of Louis XIII in 1601 and Napoleon signing his deed of abdication in 1814. As far back as the 12th century kings went hunting in the forest. The keep is the only remnant of a medieval castle.

With more than 1,500 rooms and 53ha (130 acres) of parkland, the royal château of Fontainebleau is, despite its associations with *la chasse*, no mere hunting lodge. What sets it apart is that it was the only royal and imperial residence in France to be inhabited continuously for seven centuries, and is consequently a showcase for the grander gestures of French architecture. The surviving medieval keep forms the core of the building, which was subsequently extended in splendid Renaissance style under François I and, in the 17th century, during the reign of Henri IV. A further wing was built during the time of Louis XV; after the Revolution, the château was restored by Napoleon Bonaparte. Its final royal inhabitant was Napoleon III, whose court stayed here until 1869.

The most spectacular of the interiors are the Renaissance rooms, whose rich ornament and colourful frescoes were inspired by the new artistic styles François I had seen in Italy and which proved influential in France. These rooms include the sumptuous ballroom and François I's magnificent long gallery. Altogether more intimate in scale are Marie Antoinette's boudoirs and the apartment of Louis XIV's secret second wife, Madame de Maintenon. Outside, the Grand Parterre is reputedly the largest formal garden in Europe.

Distance: 68km (42 miles)

Journey Time: 50 min

🚇 Off map ☎ 01 60 71 50 70

🕐 Château Apr–Sep Wed–Mon 9.30–6; Oct–Mar Wed–Mon 9.30–5 (last admission 45 minutes before closing). Courtyard and gardens May–Sep 9–7; Mar–Apr, Oct 9–6; Nov–Feb 9–5. Park daily 24 hours

🚃 Fontainebleau-Avon 💶 Château (limited areas only) moderate; courtyard, gardens and park free

Renaissance-style splendour at Fontainebleau

City Tours

This section contains self-guided tours that will help you explore the sights in each of the city's regions. Each tour is designed to take one or two days, with a map pinpointing the recommended places along the way. There is a quick reference guide at the end of each tour, listing everything you need in that region, so you know exactly what's close by.

Around the Tour Eiffel

Long vistas and grandiose public buildings characterize this part of Paris—but at its heart the Eiffel Tower is 324m (1,063ft) of pure, unmissable fun.

Morning

Start in front of the **Musée d'Orsay** (▷ 36–37), but save the museum itself for another day. The Musée National de la Légion d'Honneur across the street sets the tone for a walk that's rich in political and military landmarks. Continue along the quai Anatole France to the Assemblée Nationale, France's lower house of parliament, its dignified neoclassical portico facing the **place de la Concorde** (▷ 50–51) across the river. Continue along quai d'Orsay past the mansion-like ministry of foreign affairs, popularly known by its address and one of the most important architectural monuments of the Second Empire. Until 1973 it was also a residence for high officials; King Juan Carlos of Spain was the last to stay there. Admire the florid, gilded statuary of the **pont Alexandre III** (▷ 73) before turning left down broad, stately avenue du Maréchal Galliéni, named for a World War I military commander. Ahead of you is the wide, imposing facade of **Les Invalides** (▷ 68–69)—built by Louis XIV and the last resting place of Napoleon Bonaparte.

Late morning

Take time to explore the **Musée de l'Armée** (▷ 68), which occupies much of the majestic Les Invalides, before visiting France's national military pantheon, the **Église du Dôme** (▷ 68), in which Napoleon's tomb takes pride of place.

Lunch

There's a simple but strategically located café on the south side of the Musée de l'Armée, but for a more substantial lunch in elegant surroundings make a short detour to the **Brasserie Thoumieux** (▷ 145) in rue Saint-Dominique.

Afternoon

Stroll the short distance along avenue de Tourville to reach the enormous École Militaire, constructed during the time of Louis XV and still occupied by the military. It faces the **parc du Champs de Mars** (▷ 72–73), a vast green space stretching northwest towards the Eiffel Tower. To reach the park, cross the broad cobbled avenue de la Motte-Picquet with care. Amble the length of the Champs de Mars to reach the **Eiffel Tower** (▷ 60–61); buy your tickets in advance online to save time queuing.

Late afternoon

No visit to the Eiffel Tower is complete without crossing the river to experience the classic view of the tower itself. Cross the pont d'Iéna to reach the **Palais de Chaillot** (▷ 72); save its museums for another day, but go up to the piazza between the two curved wings of the complex for the best view.

Evening

Stick around until after dusk to experience the beauty of the tower's soft golden lighting—and the excitement of the 20,000 flashing lights that make it glitter for five minutes every hour on the hour.

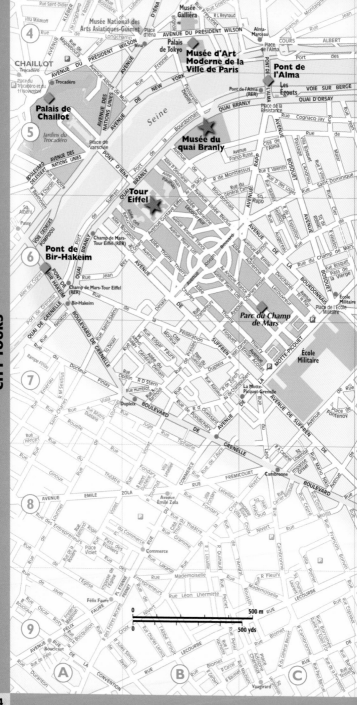

Rue Saint-Didier
Villa Malakoff
Rue Boissière
KLÉBER
Rue de Lübeck
Rue de Belloy
Rue Greuze
Musée Galliéra
Rue F. Ponchez
Rue Goethe
R Reynaud
Rue Montaigne
Jean
Montagne

Musée National des
Arts Asiatiques-Guimet
Longchamp
AVENUE DU PRÉSIDENT WILSON
Place d'Iéna
Iéna
Palais
de Tokyo
Musée d'Art
Moderne de la
Ville de Paris
Alma-
Marceau
COURS
ALBERT
Place
de l'Alma
Rue

Rue
AVENUE
DU
CHAILLOT
Trocadéro
PRÉSIDENT WILSON
AVENUE Albert de Mun
Rue de New York
Rue
Fresnel
Pont
des
Pont de
l'Alma
Place du
Trocadéro et du
11 Novembre
Trocadéro
AVENUE DES NATIONS UNIES
Les
Égouts
VOIE SUR BERGE
Pont de l'Alma
(RER)
QUAI D'ORSAY

Palais de
Chaillot
Seine
QUAI BRANLY
Place de la
Résistance
Rue
Cognacq-Jay

Jardins du
Trocadéro
Rue
des
Bourdonnais
Place de
Varsovie
Musée du
quai Branly
AVENUE
Cité de
l'Alma
Rue
Passage
l'Alma

BOULEVARD
DELESSERT
AVENUE DES NATIONS UNIES
PONT D'IÉNA
Port
Branly
Allée des Refuzniks
Avenue
Franco-Russe
RAPP
Rue
Bosquet
Rue
Saint-Dominique

VOIE GEORGES
POMPIDOU
Sq.
Albini
Patsy
QUAI
BRANLY
Rue
R. de Monttessuy
Rue du
Général Camou
Avenue
Élisée Reclus
AVENUE
Rue E. Valentin
Rue D. des Loges
Rue
Rue
Rue St-Dominique

Tour
Eiffel
Champ de Mars-
Tour Eiffel (RER)
Avenue Gustave Eiffel
Allée Adrienne Lecouvreur
Avenue
Anatole France
RAPP
Avenue
Rue
Rue
Rue
Rue

Pont de
Bir-Hakeim
PONT DE BIR-HAKEIM
Quai
Rue
Jean
Allée Thomy Thierry
AVENUE
DE
Allée Jean Paulhan
Avenue Joseph Bouvard
Avenue Charles Risler
Avenue de la
Bourdonnais
Rue du Champ de Mars
Rue Bosquet
Pass. de
la Vierge

Allée des Cygnes
Champ de Mars-Tour Eiffel
(RER)
Bir-Hakeim
Rue Saint-Saëns
Avenue Octave Gréard
Avenue Charles Floquet
Avenue Pierre Loti
Avenue Elisée Reclus
Avenue
Silvestre de Sacy
Avenue
de la Motte-Picquet
Parc du Champ
de Mars
École
Militaire
Place de l'École
Militaire
Pont de Grenelle
QUAI DE GRENELLE
Rue Nélaton
BOULEVARD DE GRENELLE
Cité
Martel
Fédération
SUFFREN
AVENUE
École
Militaire
Rue
du
Docteur
Finlay
Rue
Sextius
Michel
Rue Edgar Faure
Allée du Général Detrie
Rue
Général
Ferrié
Duquesne
MOTTE-PICQUET
AVENUE
DE
SUFFREN

Rampe Finlay
Rue
Viala
Rue
Humblot
R D Stern
Rue Clodion
Rue
Duplex
Place
Dupleix
Rue
Dupleix
La Motte
Picquet-Grenelle
Place de
Fontenoy

Rue
Émeriau
Rue
R M Sextius
Rue Maria
Deraismes
Dupleix
BOULEVARD
Rue de
Pondichéry
DE
AVENUE
DE
LA MOTTE-PICQUET
Rue
de
Lourmel
GRENELLE
Rue
Laos
Impasse
Créisel
Cambronne

Rue
Rue
Ginoux
Rue
Théâtre
Rue Rouelle
Rue
Hilaire
buisson
Villa
Leblanc
Villa
Letellier
COMMERCE
RUE
Rue
Lecourbe
FRÉMICOURT
Sq.
Saint-
Lambert
Rue
Blomet
Rue
Nivert
Rue
BOULEVARD

Rue
Hélicart
AVENUE
ÉMILE
ZOLA
Fondary
Rue
Viclot
Avenue
Émile Zola
du Commerce
Cité
Trévise
Rue Lakanal
RUE
Rue
Fondary
Croix
Nivert
Rue
Rue
Sq. Jean
Rostand
Miollis
Nivert
Cambronne
Villa
Bonieu
Villa
Santos-Dumont

Rue
des
Entrepreneurs
Rue
Violet
Rue
Roger
Bacon
Pass. des
Écoliers
Place
Violet
Commerce
RUE
Rue Gramme
R. Fallempin
Rue Mademoiselle
R Ouinault
Rue
Rue
R Fleury
Mademoiselle
Rue
LECOURBE
Place
Cambronne

Rue de
l'Église
Rue Félix Faure
Impasse
Fernet
R. Étienne
Pernet
Rue
Rue Entrepreneurs
Rue Léon Lhermitte
Rue
Péclet
Rue
de
l'Abbé
Groult
Rue Léon
Rue des
Frères Morane
Rue
Carcel
Rue du Général
Guilhem
Rue
de
Vaugirard

AVENUE
Rue Oscar Roty
Félix Faure
Bouicaut
Rue de Javel
FAURE
RUE
Rue
Saint-Charles
Rue
Bargue
Rue des Volontaires
Rue
Blomet
Blomet
Rue
Perel
Place
Adolphe
Chérioux
RUE

Rue
Duranton
AVENUE
Rue de Javel
Boucicaut
Rue de
Pâtis
DE
LA
CONVENTION
Rue
Jules Simon
Rue Bocquillon
R L'Abbé Groult
L'Abbé
Groult
Rue Charles Lecocq
Rue Bargue
Rue Castagnary
Rue du Général
Guilhem
RUE
DE
Vaugirard

0   500 m
0   500 yds

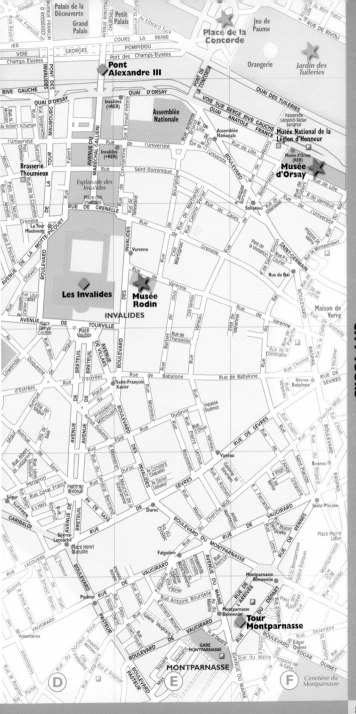

Around the Tour Eiffel
Quick Reference Guide

TOP 25 SIGHTS AND EXPERIENCES

Musée d'Orsay (▷ 36)
The architectural merit of this auda-cious conversion of a former railway station still divides opinion, but its breathtaking collection makes it one of Paris's must-see attractions.

Musée du quai Branly (▷ 40)
The national collection of art from Africa, Asia, Oceania and the Americas is housed in a modernist building by superstar architect Jean Nouvel and set in luxuriant gardens.

Musée Rodin (▷ 42)
An 18th-century mansion and its peaceful garden provide the set-ting for the sculptures left to the nation by Rodin, along with other works by him and contemporaries.

Tour Eiffel (▷ 60)
Though it was originally built as a temporary structure for the 1889 Exposition Universelle, it's hard to imagine Paris now without Gustave Eiffel's instantly recognizable tower.

CITY TOURS

Viewing the Seine on the Pont des Arts

Latin Quarter, St-Germain and Islands

The Left Bank's literary and philosophical associations lend intellectual lustre to this tour; fashion and fine dining bring Parisian élan to the mix; and the loveliness of the Seine and its islands adds a final dash of romance.

Morning

Start at rue Mouffetard, where the wonderful food and wine shops ensure a bustling atmosphere from morning onwards. Make your way to the church of **Saint Étienne-du-Mont** (▷ 67), worth a quick peek for its flamboyant late Gothic choir, before visiting the **Panthéon** (▷ 72), whose stately neoclassical dome dominates the Latin Quarter—Paris's university district. A gentle stroll down rue Soufflot brings you to the main entrance to the **Jardin du Luxembourg** (▷ 22–23). Do as the locals do and read in the sun.

Mid-morning

Leave the park by the exit on busy rue de Vaugirard, then follow the gently curving rue Servandoni and rue Palatine to reach **Église Saint-Sulpice** (▷ 68), another Left Bank church well worth a look—this time for its cathedral-like internal dimensions. From here to the boulevard St-Germain the streets are full of intriguing boutiques; indulge in a spot of window-shopping at **Marie Mercié** (▷ 128) or **Sonia Rykiel** (▷ 129), or polish your intellectual credentials in the wonderful bookshop **La Hune** (▷ 126). Burnish them further with a pick-me-up on the terrace of **Café Les Deux Magots** (▷ 66) or **Café de Flore** (▷ 66)— these famous cafés were once the haunts of existentialists and authors.

Late morning

The church of **Saint-Germain-des-Prés** (▷ 67) gives its name to one of Paris's most atmospheric quarters, wedged between boulevard St-Germain and the river. The streets are lined with handsome old houses and dotted with small art galleries and antiques shops; tucked into pretty rue Furstenberg is the Musée National Eugène Delacroix.

Lunch

This is an excellent part of town in which to break for lunch. Choose between the big brasserie buzz of **Alcazar** (▷ 144), the hip fusion cuisine of **Ze Kitchen Galerie** (▷ 151) or the view from **Le Ciel de Paris** (▷ 146).

Afternoon

Follow rue Dauphine to the **pont Neuf** (▷ 74), crossing to the Île de la Cité to soak up the sun in the beautiful **square du Vert-Galant** (▷ 75), a tiny park on the island's western tip that offers wonderful views along the Seine. Afterwards, skirt the Île's north bank past the brooding bulk of the **Conciergerie** (▷ 18–19), a former royal palace, fortress and prison. Like the church of **Sainte-Chapelle** (▷ 56–57), it now forms part of the Palais de Justice. Slow the pace to admire the colours of the **Marché aux Fleurs** (▷ 128) before turning down rue de la Cité to reach the cathedral of **Notre-Dame** (▷ 44–45).

Late afternoon

Visiting the cathedral is free, but there's a charge to climb the towers, so leave this for another day. Instead, admire the flying buttresses from ground level before pausing at the sombre **Mémorial des Martyrs de la Déportation**.

Evening

The soft light of evening casts a particularly alluring spell over the **Île Saint-Louis** (▷ 68), for many visitors one of Paris's most romantic corners. Stroll its embankments to enjoy views of Notre-Dame and the Seine before crossing back to the Left Bank for dinner at **La Tour d'Argent** (▷ 151).

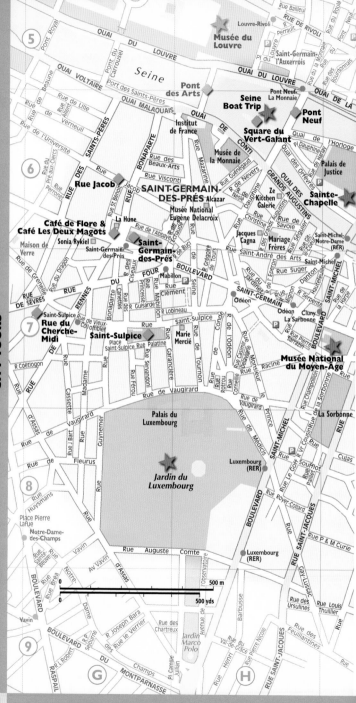

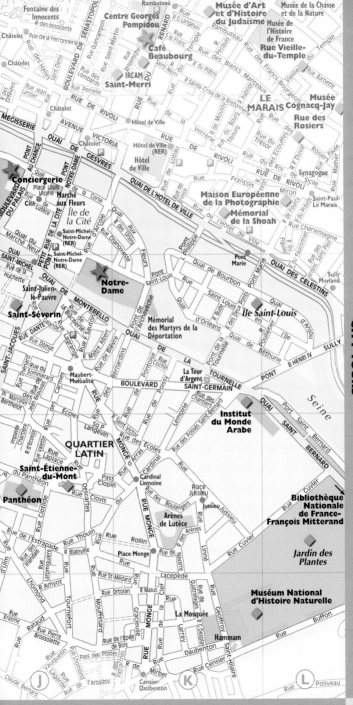

Rambuteau

Fontaine des Innocents
R. des Innocents

Musée d'Art et d'Histoire du Judaïsme

Musée de la Chasse et de la Nature

Centre Georges Pompidou

Châtelet

Rue de la Ferronnerie

Musée de l'Histoire de France

Rue Vieille-du-Temple

Café Beaubourg

Châtelet

IRCAM

Saint-Merri

LE MARAIS

Musée Cognacq-Jay

Rue des Rosiers

Hôtel de Ville

AVENUE VICTORIA

Châtelet

RUE DE RIVOLI

Hôtel de Ville (RER)

Hôtel de Ville

RUE DE RIVOLI

RUE DE RIVOLI

Synagogue
Saint-Paul-Le Marais

MÉGISSERIE

QUAI DE GESVRES

QUAI DE L'HOTEL DE VILLE

Conciergerie

Place Louis Lépine

Marché aux Fleurs

Île de la Cité

Maison Européenne de la Photographie

Mémorial de la Shoah

Saint-Michel-Notre-Dame (RER)

Pont Marie

QUAI DES CELESTINS

Sully Morland

Notre-Dame

Saint-Julien-le-Pauvre

Saint-Séverin

MONTEBELLO

Mémorial des Martyrs de la Déportation

Île Saint-Louis

Maubert-Mutualité

BOULEVARD

La Tour d'Argent

SAINT-GERMAIN

PONT B. HENRI IV

SULLY

Seine

Institut du Monde Arabe

QUARTIER LATIN

QUAI SAINT BERNARD

Cardinal Lemoine

Place Jussieu

Jussieu

Saint-Étienne-du-Mont

Bibliothèque Nationale de France-François Mitterand

Panthéon

Arènes de Lutèce

RUE MONGE

Place Monge

Jardin des Plantes

Rollin

La Mosquée

Muséum National d'Histoire Naturelle

Hammam

Censier-Daubenton

Rue Censier

Poliveau

J K L

CITY TOURS

Latin Quarter, St-Germain and Islands
Quick Reference Guide

SIGHTS AND EXPERIENCES

Conciergerie (▷ 18)
Part medieval palace, part prison, this impressive but grim place preserves poignant memories of the victims of the French Revolution, including Marie Antoinette.

Jardin du Luxembourg (▷ 22)
The epitome of French landscaping, this garden was commissioned by Marie de Médicis in 1615 and designed to remind her of her childhood Florentine home.

Musée National du Moyen-Âge (▷ 34)
A turreted 15th-century mansion provides an appropriate setting for the national collection of medieval and Gothic art.

Notre-Dame (▷ 44)
Gargoyles, flying buttresses and a 93m (305ft) spire enrich the exterior of this famous cathedral; climb the towers to see its dramatic Gothic architecture up close.

Sainte-Chapelle (▷ 56)
Hidden within the Palais de Justice is a delicate late Gothic gem: Louis IX's soaring royal chapel, with a star-studded roof and breathtaking stained glass.

Seine Boat Trip (▷ 58)
Your feet will appreciate the rest as you watch the most important sights of Paris float gently by on a romantic one-hour boat trip along the River Seine.

CITY TOURS

93

Marais and Bastille

Contemporary art meets high fashion in Paris's trendiest district, yet alongside the *branché* boutiques and bars the Marais preserves magnificent architecture and its continuing role as the focus of the city's Jewish life.

Morning

Start with a late breakfast on the terrace at the chic **Café Beaubourg** (▷ 66) and ponder the still-audacious design of the **Centre Georges Pompidou** (▷ 16–17), which caused quite a stir with its exposed ductwork and glass-roofed escalators when it first opened in 1977. Today isn't the day to visit; instead, admire the jaunty Fontaine Stravinsky before walking the length of the museum, turning right into rue Rambuteau to reach the **Musée d'Art et d'Histoire du Judaïsme** (▷ 69–70) on rue du Temple. Housed in a grand 17th-century mansion or *hôtel particulier*, the museum documents European Jewish history and art from the Middle Ages onwards.

Late morning

Rue Rambuteau runs into rue des Francs-Bourgeois, graced by more aristocratic town houses. Turn left up **rue Vieille-du-Temple** (▷ 75) to discover some of the Marais's hip designer stores, including **Vanessa Bruno** (▷ 129) at No.100 and **Surface 2 Air** (▷ 129) at No.108. Turn right into rue Debelleyme and right again to reach the **Musée Picasso** (▷ 38–39), housed in another mansion, the elegant Hôtel Salé. Continue along rue Thorigny to rue Elzévir, where the 16th-century Hôtel Donon houses the **Musée Cognacq-Jay** (▷ 70–71), whose 18th-century paintings and *objets d'art* were assembled by the owner of the Samaritaine department store. Returning to rue des Francs-Bourgeois, the **Hôtel Carnavalet** (▷ 28) also dates from the 16th century and comprises one half of Paris's splendid museum of local history, **Musée Carnavalet** (▷ 28). Admire the architecture, but save the interior for another day.

Lunch

If the Marais's trendy shops have drained your funds, the inexpensive Jewish restaurants along **rue des Rosiers** (▷ 75) will be a welcome sight. **L'As du Fallafel** (▷ 144) at No. 34 is generally reckoned to serve the best falafel (mashed chickpeas formed into a ball and deep fried) in the city, but don't come here on Saturday—it's closed.

Afternoon

Retrace your steps to rue des Francs-Bourgeois, continuing as far as **place des Vosges** (▷ 52–53). This beautiful formal square dates from the early 17th century and is the best preserved in Paris; in the southeast corner, Victor Hugo's house is now a museum. Rue de Birague leads from the south side of the square to busy rue Saint-Antoine; to the left is the place de la Bastille, former site of the infamous prison and now dominated by the ultramodern **Opéra Bastille** (▷ 138). To the right, the Hôtel de Béthune-Sully is among the most magnificent of all the Marais's mansions; you can't visit the interior—now occupied by the Ministry of Culture—but you can admire the court and elegant garden. Continue along rue Saint-Antoine and rue François-Miron to reach the **Mémorial de la Shoah** (▷ 69), on rue Geoffroy l'Asnier—a sombre counterpoint to the **Musée d'Art et d'Histoire du Judaïsme**.

Dinner

Bofinger (▷ 145) is one of Paris's most historic brasseries and a memorable spot for dinner. Afterwards, stay in the Marais for a drink in one of the area's lively cafés and bars—many of them popular with the city's gay and lesbian community.

La Bourse
LA BOURSE
Bourse
Rue Beauregard
Rue Poissonnière
Strasbourg
Saint-Denis
R Sainte-Apolline
Rue du Croissant
Rue des Jeuneurs
d'Aboukir
Pass Lemoine
R Blondel
Rue Saint-Joseph
Rue Sainte-Foy
Rue Saint-Foy
Rue d'Alexandrie
R de Tracy
Rue du Mail
Rue Léopold Bellan
d Petits Carreaux
Rue Dussoubs
Passage du Ponceau
R Papin
Sentier
Rue d'Aboukir
Sentier
RUE REAUMUR
Reaumur
Sébastopol
Place des Victoires
Rue Bachaumont
Rue Saint-Sauveur
Pass Palestro
Musée des Arts et Métiers
Rue Mandar
Greneta
Pass du Grand Cerf
Rue Coq Héron Louvre
RUE ETIENNE
Rue Marie Stuart
Tiquetonne
LES HALLES
RUE DE TURBIGO

Galerie Vivienne

Galerie Véro-Dodat

Saint-Eustache
Les Halles
Jardin du Forum des Halles
Forum des Halles
Étienne Marcel (RER)

Centre Georges Pompidou

Louvre-Rivoli
RUE DE RIVOLI
Saint-Germain-l'Auxerrois
Châtelet Les Halles (RER)
Fontaine des Innocents
Châtelet
Rue de la Ferronnerie
Rambuteau
Café Beaubourg
IRCAM
Saint-Merri

Seine Boat Trip
Square du Vert-Galant
Pont Neuf La Monnaie
Pont Neuf
QUAI DU LOUVRE
QUAI DE LA MÉGISSERIE
Châtelet
RUE DE RIVOLI
Hôtel de Ville
AVENUE VICTORIA
Hôtel de Ville (RER)
Hôtel de Ville

Seine

Palais de Justice
Conciergerie
Sainte-Chapelle
La Seine
Place Louis Lépine
Marché aux Fleurs
Île de la Cité
Saint-Michel-Notre-Dame (RER)

Mariage Frères
Saint-Michel
Saint-Michel-Notre-Dame (RER)
Saint-Michel Notre-Dame (RER)
Notre-Dame

Saint-Séverin
Saint-Julien-le-Pauvre
Mémorial des Martyrs de la Déportation

Cluny
La Sorbonne

Musée National du Moyen-Âge

0   500 m
0   500 yds

BOULEVARD SAINT-GERMAIN

La Sorbonne
Maubert-Mutualité

H   J   K

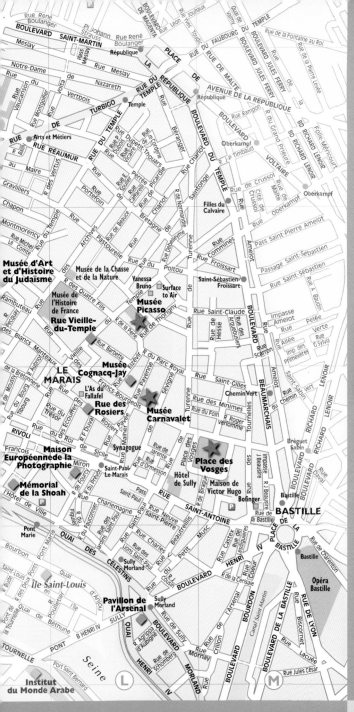

TOP 25 SIGHTS AND EXPERIENCES

Centre Georges Pompidou (▷ 16)

The museum houses the national collection of modern and contemporary art, from Fauvism, Cubism and Surrealism to Pop Art and works by the stars of the contemporary art scene. The building includes a library, cinema, bookshops and a chic restaurant.

Musée Carnavalet (▷ 28)

There is no better place to plunge into the history of Paris than the Musée Carnavalet, with period rooms and objects up to the 20th century. The section dealing with the Revolution is particularly gripping—figures such as Robespierre are brought vividly to life in their historical context.

Musée Picasso (▷ 38)

Some 500 works by Picasso are displayed in this historic Marais mansion, following a thorough refurbishment by architect Jean-François Bodin that has tripled the exhibition area and improved access for visitors with disabilities. It boasts one of the world's finest collections of work by the artist.

Place des Vosges (▷ 52)

Built on the site of a 14th-century royal palace that was abandoned and demolished by Catherine de Médicis after her husband Henri II died there, this handsome square of arcaded red-brick houses overlooks a central garden and dates from 1612. Famous former residents include Victor Hugo.

Louvre and Champs-Élysées

Dress to impress for this route through the very heart of Paris, where iconic landmarks and glamorous designer shopping ensure there's plenty of interest along the way.

Morning

Start with a late breakfast on the terrace of the **Café Marly** (▷ 146) at the **Louvre** (▷ 30–31). You'll probably want to set aside another day to see the collection but this is a fine vantage point from which to admire the splendid setting and the audacity of I. M. Pei's modernist glass pyramid. Cross the busy place du Carrousel du Louvre to reach the **Arc de Triomphe du Carrousel**—not the famous triumphal arch but a smaller version, Roman in its inspiration and built in 1805 to celebrate Napoleon's victories. Beyond it, there's a dramatic view along Paris's monumental axis—west through the **Jardin des Tuileries** (▷ 24–25), across the **place de la Concorde** (▷ 50–51) and up the avenue des Champs-Élysées to the Arc de Triomphe and the distant **Grande Arche** (▷ 76) at La Défense. The Jardin des Tuileries itself is Paris's most central park, and a UNESCO World Heritage Site since 1991. Two galleries—the **Orangerie** (▷ 51) and **Jeu de Paume** (▷ 51)—offer an excellent excuse to linger a while.

Mid-morning

Leave the Jardin des Tuileries by the rue de Castiglione exit. Admire the view up rue de Castiglione towards the elegant place Vendôme and its centrepiece—a 44m (144ft) bronze column inspired by Trajan's column in Rome—before turning left to window-shop your way along rue Saint-Honoré. The attention-seeking awnings of Galliano's store, patterned with newsprint, are visible on the right before rue Royale. Crossing rue Royale admire the neoclassical facade of the **Église de la Madeleine**, originally built as a monument to Napoleon's army but nowadays a fashionable place of worship. Beyond rue Royale, rue Saint-Honoré becomes **rue du Faubourg Saint-Honoré** (▷ 74), home to the Élysée palace—official residence of the French president— and to some of Paris's most luxurious designer boutiques. Avenue Matignon continues the luxury theme but with fine art galleries and antique dealers in place of fashion; the art deco furniture and lighting on display at **Makassar France** at No.19 are particularly eye-catching.

Lunch
The chic 8th *arrondissement* offers plenty of good options for an elegant lunch; **6 New York** (▷ 144) or **Spoon** (▷ 150) are both suitably stylish, contemporary choices.

Afternoon
The window-shopping shifts up a gear on the far side of the Rond Point des Champs-Élysées along avenue Montaigne. Here, **Dior** (▷ 125) and **Chanel** (▷ 124) both have splendid flagship stores in which to lose half a day, and the array of designer labels is enough to constitute a serious hazard to your bank balance. Turn right off avenue Montaigne up rue François 1er to reach the broad avenue des Champs-Élysées, Paris's most famous boulevard, which ends at place de l'Étoile and is dominated by the stately bulk of the **Arc de Triomphe** (▷ 14–15). Quite aside from its significance as a national monument, the Arc also makes an excellent platform for views across the city.

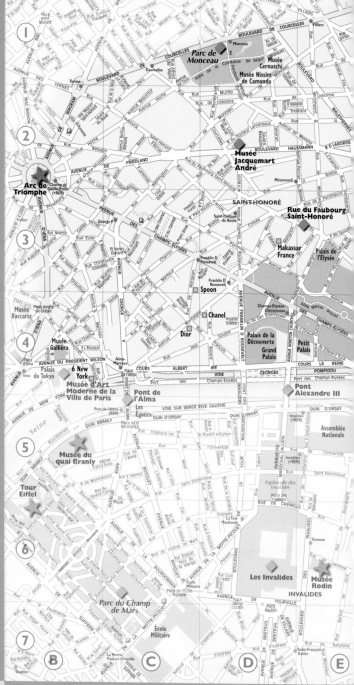

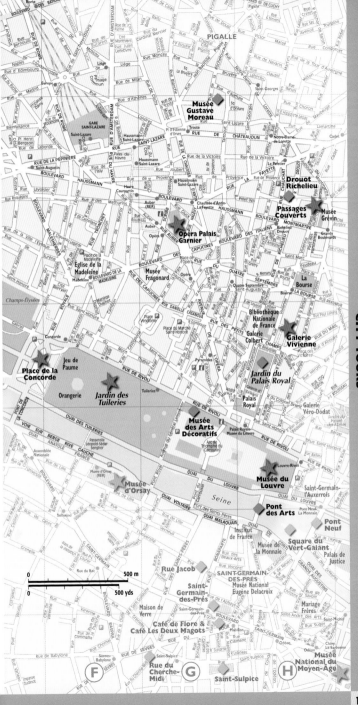

PIGALLE

Musée Gustave Moreau

Drouot Richelieu

Passages Couverts

Musée Grévin

Opéra Palais Garnier

Eglise de la Madeleine

Musée Fragonard

La Bourse

Bibliothèque Nationale de France

Galerie Colbert

Galerie Vivienne

Place de la Concorde

Jeu de Paume

Orangerie

Jardin des Tuileries

Jardin du Palais Royal

Palais Royal

Galerie Véro-Dodat

Musée des Arts Décoratifs

Arc de triomphe du Carrousel

Musée du Louvre

Musée d'Orsay

Saint-Germain-l'Auxerrois

Pont des Arts

Pont Neuf

Square du Vert-Galant

Palais de Justice

Rue Jacob

SAINT-GERMAIN-DES-PRÉS
Musée National Eugène Delacroix

Mariage Frères

Saint-Germain-des-Prés

Maison de Verre

Café de Flore & Café Les Deux Magots

Cluny La Sorbonne

Rue du Cherche-Midi

Saint-Sulpice

Musée National du Moyen-Age

F   **G**   **H**

0 ——— 500 m
0 ——— 500 yds

Louvre and Champs-Élysées
Quick Reference Guide

CITY TOURS

Arc de Triomphe (▷ 14)
With 12 of Haussmann's avenues radiating from it, this arch is the focus of national pride and a memorial to France's war dead, with a Memorial Flame at its base.

Galerie Vivienne and the Passages Couverts (▷ 20)
A network of 19th-century shopping arcades allows you to stroll and people watch under cover.

Jardin des Tuileries (▷ 24)
One of the most popular parks for Parisians was first laid out in the 16th century and is a delightful place in which to relax.

Musée du Louvre (▷ 30)
The world's largest museum is a dazzling experience, from the modernist glass pyramid over its entrance to its world-famous treasures.

Opéra Palais Garnier (▷ 46)
Charles Garnier's wedding cake of a building is as sumptuous as an opera house should be, with a foyer and grand staircase every bit as majestic as the auditorium itself.

Place de la Concorde (▷ 50)
A maelstrom of traffic today, this vast open space has a violent past, as the site of the gruesome guillotine during the French Revolution.

CITY TOURS

105

Montmartre

Art meets raffish nightlife, picturesque views and stepped streets in this still remarkably village-like corner of the city.

Morning
Wear comfortable shoes—the route is mostly downhill and avoids steps as far as possible, but this is still the highest point in the city, the slopes can be steep and the streets are cobbled in places. Take the Métro to Abbesses station; it's the city's deepest, with a lovely original art nouveau canopy. Window-shop your way from **place des Abbesses** (▷ 73) past small, funky boutiques in rue Yvonne le Tac and rue Tardieu to reach the funicular. One of the area's celebrated stepped streets runs parallel to it, but the railway is easier on your feet. Journey's end is the distinctive, white hilltop basilica of **Sacré-Cœur** (▷ 54–55). It's one of Paris's most visited attractions and the crush inside can sometimes mar the experience. What doesn't disappoint is the breathtaking view over the city—whether from the dome or from the terrace in front of the church.

Late morning
Follow rue du Cardinal Guibert along the side of the church, braving the tourist hubbub of rue Chevalier de la Barre to reach calmer, prettier rue Cortot. Here, the **Musée de Montmartre** (▷ 71) documents the history and artistic associations of the area, which in the 19th century became a popular place of entertainment. Continue along rue Cortot to the junction with rue des Saules—if you haven't already caught a glimpse of Montmartre's vineyard, it's just downhill to the right. Turn uphill along rue des Saules then left into rue Norvins to reach bustling place du Tertre, famous for its portrait painters.

Lunch

This is an unashamedly touristy part of Montmartre, with no shortage of places to eat, though of variable quality; **Au Clair de la Lune** (▷ 145) in rue Poulbot is one of the nicest options, tucked away off place du Tertre close to the Espace Montmartre Salvador Dalí, which has a permanent collection of 300 of the Surrealist artist's works.

Afternoon

From rue Poulbot, turn left down rue Norvins to reach the Radet, the first of Montmartre's windmills, at the top of rue Lepic; there were once 14 but now this and the nearby Blute Fin are the last survivors. Together they constitute the **Moulin de la Galette**, which during its time as a dance hall was painted by Renoir. It is now a restaurant. Continue downhill on rue Lepic, turning sharply right at its junction with rue des Abbesses to reach the **Cimetière de Montmartre** (▷ 66–67), where the roll call of famous names rivals that of Père Lachaise.

Evening

Rue des Abbesses and the surrounding streets hum with life in the evening; catch a film at **Studio 28** (▷ 139), enjoy dinner at **Café Burq** (▷ 146) or dinner and a show at **Michou** (▷ 138). Later and live-lier nightlife—from rock concerts to discos and sleazy sex clubs—is found at the foot of rue des Martyrs on place Pigalle and boulevard de Clichy, the latter dominated by the famous **Moulin Rouge** (▷ 138) club.

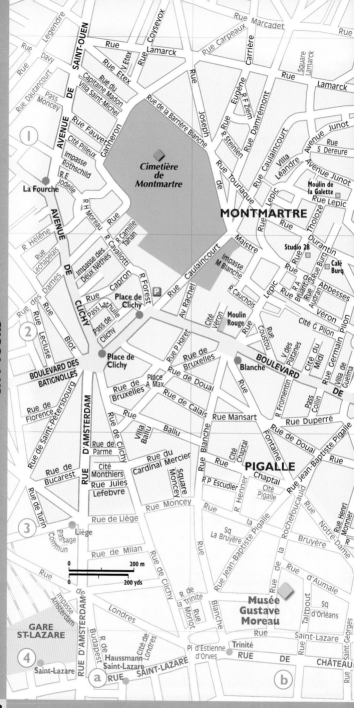

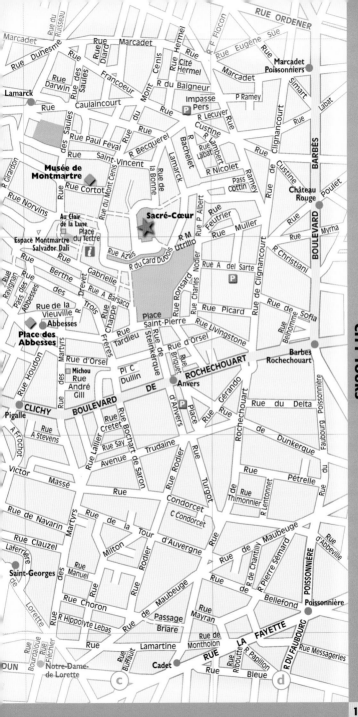

Montmartre Quick Reference Guide

SIGHTS AND EXPERIENCES

Sacré-Cœur (▷ 54)

Neo-Romanesque and Byzantine in style, the white basilica of Sacré-Cœur is one of the most familiar features of the Parisian skyline, looking down on the city from its lofty hilltop perch. Built as a memorial to the 58,000 dead of the Franco-Prussian war, it wasn't completed until the eve of World War I and was only consecrated in 1919. Its lovely stained-glass windows were destroyed during World War II and restored afterwards.

MORE TO SEE   64

Cimetière de Montmartre   Place des Abbesses
Musée de Montmartre

The interior of Sacré-Cœur

CITY TOURS

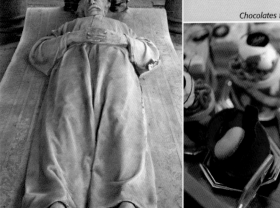

Tomb of Alexandre Dumas in the Cimetière de Montmartre

Chocolates for sale

Further Afield

Louis XIV's palace at Versailles is one excursion not to miss, while more offbeat charm is to be found in the outer *arrondissements* of the city's north and east.

DAY 1
Morning

Take RER line C to Versailles Rive Gauche and stroll the short distance to the **Château de Versailles** (▷ 62–63). Try for an early start—the château opens at 9—and buy your ticket online to skip the worst of the queues. Start with the Grands Appartements: admire the bombastic painted ceiling of the Hall of Mirrors, which celebrates Louis's military campaigns, before visiting the opulent Queen's Chamber.

Lunch

If you're visiting at the weekend between April and October, exit into the gardens before midday to catch the Grandes Eaux fountains performing to music; they perform again from 3.30 to 5.30. Afterwards, stroll down to the Grand Canal where there are formal and informal lunch options—La Flottille (tel 1 39 51 41 58; www.laflottille.fr) has a garden terrace by the waterside.

Afternoon

Follow the route marked on the free map to reach the **Petit Trianon** (▷ 63). Closely associated with Marie Antoinette, this charming country estate is for many the highlight of a visit to Versailles. Explore the twee Hameau de la Reine—a play village built for the queen's amusement—before continuing through formal gardens to reach the **Grand Trianon** (▷ 63), the colonnaded marble palace where Louis XIV enjoyed trysts with his mistress, Madame de Montespan.

DAY 2
Morning
Another early start, this time for a weekend stroll through the **Marché aux Puces de St-Ouen** (▷ 26–27)—Paris's most famous flea market. Take Métro line 4 to Porte de Clignancourt and cross under the Périphérique to get there by 10. Fortify yourself with coffee from one of the cafés along rue des Rosiers and pick up a free map from the tourist office at 7 impasse Simon by the Marché Paul Bert to navigate your way. Spend a couple of hours to appreciate the sheer variety on offer, from second-hand clothes to elegant art deco furniture and fine art.

Lunch
Take the Métro to Barbès Rochechouart, change to line 2 (direction: Nation) and alight at Stalingrad. Admire the 18th-century Rotonde de la Villette and the views up the canal basin towards **parc de la Villette** (▷ 76) before climbing hilly avenue Sécretan. Assemble a picnic from the covered market and shops here. Eat it in the **parc des Buttes Chaumont** (▷ 76) at the top of the hill—if you're lucky, you might get one of its hillocks to yourself.

Afternoon
Descend avenue Mathurin Moreau to Colonel Fabien station. Take the Métro to Père Lachaise—there's a gate into the **Cimetière du Père-Lachaise** (▷ 48–49) directly opposite, but the main entrance is further along boulevard de Ménilmontant. Pick up a map to find the most-visited graves, including those of Oscar Wilde, Édith Piaf and Jim Morrison, but be sure to admire the extraordinary architecture of the many tombs, too.

Early evening
Stay in the area for an apéritif or relaxed early dinner in trendy rue Oberkampf. **Le Styx** (▷ 151) is an informal, inexpensive choice in this hip area.

La Grande Arche

LA DÉFENSE

A14

BD DE VERDUN

QUAI DU MARECHAL JOFFRE

D7

Seine

BOULEVARD JEAN JAURES

RUE MARTRE D19

BOULEVARD

Île de la Grande Jatte

D909

AVENUE DE

D908

BOULEVARD BINEAU

AVENUE CHARLES DE GAULLE

N13

BOULEVARD MALESHERBES

17

Parc de Monceau

Mare Saint-James

D1

ALLÉE DE LONGCHAMP

Ruisseau de Longchamp

BOULEVARD PÉRIPHÉRIQUE

Lac Inférieur

8   ST-HONORÉ

AVENUE DES CHAMPS-ÉLYSÉES

AVENUE VICTOR HUGO

CHAILLOT

QUAI BRANLY

QUAI D' ORSAY

Esplanade des Invalides

Bois de Boulogne

★ 16
Musée Marmottan Monet

Parc du Champ de Mars

Lac Supérieur

BD DE GRENELLE

INVALIDES

7

RUE DE

E05

AVENUE DE VERSAILLES

QUAI ANDRÉ CITROËN

RUE DE LA CONVENTION

RUE LECOURBE

BOULEVARD MURAT

ROUTE DE LA REINE

Seine

✦ **Parc André-Citroën**

DE

VAUGIRARD

15   MONTPARNASSE

RUE

Parc Georges Brassens

QUAI DU PONT DU JOUR

Parc Suzanne Lenglen

Parc Departemental de l'île Saint-Germain

D76

D989

BOULEVARD LEFEBVRE

BOULEVARD BRUNE

BOULEVARD PÉRIPHÉRIQUE

★
Versailles

Île Saint-Germain

QUAI DE STALINGRAD

D989

D71

Parc Frederic Pic

AVENUE DE PARIS

D906

D50

0   1 km

0   1 mile

↑ **Chantilly**

SEINE-ST-DENIS

Cimetière Parisien de St-Ouen

Marché aux Puces de Saint-Ouen ★

BOULEVARD PÉRIPHÉRIQUE

Cimetière Parisien de Pantin-Bobigny

BOULEVARD NEY

RUE ORDENER

Parc de la Villette 🌳

MONTMARTRE

Cimetière de Montmartre

18

Bassin de la Villette

19

Parc de la Butte Rouge

PIGALLE

Parc des Buttes Chaumont 🌳

9   10

RUE DE BELLEVILLE

BOULEVARD HAUSSMANN

Parc de Belleville

PARIS

2

RÉPUBLIQUE

20

Le Styx ▢

LES HALLES

3

Jardin des Tuileries

Jardin du Palais Royal

Cimetière du Père-Lachaise ★

1

LE MARAIS

RUE OBERKAMPF

ST-GERMAIN-DES-PRÉS

Île de la Cité

4

BOULEVARD VOLTAIRE

Île Saint-Louis

BASTILLE

11

Jardin du Luxembourg

6

BOULEVARD DIDEROT

QUARTIER LATIN

Jardin des Plantes

12

Cimetière du Montparnasse

5

Parc de Bercy

BERCY

BOULEVARD ARAGO

BD VINCENT AURIOL

QUAI DE BERCY

BOULEVARD PONIATOWSKI

14

13

TOLBIAC

Parc Montsouris

BOULEVARD JOURDAN

Parc Kellerman

BOULEVARD MASSENA

Disneyland®Resort Paris

AUTOROUTE DU SOLEIL

↙ **Fontainebleau**

TOP 25 SIGHTS AND EXPERIENCES

CITY TOURS

Marché aux Puces de Saint-Ouen (▷ 26)

The sprawling, 7ha (15-acre) Marché aux Puces de St-Ouen is not one market but a series of market buildings, arcades, stalls and individual dealers that together create an enjoyable way to spend a weekend morning in the city alongside the locals.

Musée Marmottan Monet (▷ 32)

This 19th-century mansion is an elegant setting for a truly mesmerising collection of Impressionist canvases, including Monet's memorable and world-renowned canvases of dappled irises, wisteria and water lilies from his last years at Giverny.

Père Lachaise (▷ 48)

The chance to see the tombs of literary, musical and artistic greats—including Frederick Chopin, Marcel Proust and of course, Oscar Wilde—is what draws many visitors to this hilly, historic cemetery, but the wonderful architecture of its myriad tombs and vaults repays languid exploration.

Versailles (▷ 62)

The pomp and grandeur of the Sun King, Louis XIV, survives in swaggering stone form at the Château de Versailles, but the complex also offers more intimate glimpses of royal life at the estates of Grand and Petit Trianon. Despite the crowds its rural idyll makes for a perfect day out from the city rush.

Modern design on a huge scale, La Grand Arche

Shop

Whether you're looking for the best local products, a department store or a quirky boutique, you'll find them all in Paris. In this section shops are listed alphabetically.

SHOP

Introduction

One of the world's shopping meccas, Paris is not all about luxury designer stores. Don't forget the individual shops, inexpensive chain stores, big and small flea markets and everything in between.

The Capital of Fashion

Narrow rue du Faubourg Saint-Honoré and broad, stately avenue Montaigne are the most prestigious fashion addresses in the city—the places to go for couture, luxury and high price tags, or simply for a spot of *lèche-vitrines* (window-shopping) past the beautiful displays. In these streets you'll find the top names—Gucci, Roberto Cavalli and Prada. Rue de la Paix glitters with names, including Cartier and Van Cleef et Arpels. To the north are the great belle époque department stores of boulevard Haussmann, Galeries Lafayette and Printemps, complete with English-speaking hostesses.

Nip across the Seine to Saint-Germain-des-Prés for fashion with flair alongside fine art and antiques and, further south, the city's oldest department store, Le Bon Marché (▷ 123), at 24 rue de Sèvres.

The Capital of Chic

Be sure not to miss the historic *arrondissements* between the Louvre and Bastille. Fashion has colonized the area around place des Victoires in the 1st with Marc Jacobs and

GOURMET PICNICS

There isn't a word for delicatessen in French. A *charcuterie* is a pork butcher and a *traiteur* a caterer, or a shop selling ready-cooked dishes. The two are closely related and are often combined. Inside, glass cabinets or counters display dozens of exquisite freshly prepared salads, grated carrots, paper-thin slices of cucumber, aubergines (eggplant), mushrooms, meat pies and spicy sausages, as well as garlic, bean-and-pork stew and a gourmet mix of cooked meats.

Clockwise from top: Tasty choices at Le Bon Marché Rive Gauche; macaroons from Ladurée pâtisserie; sweet treats from Stohrer chocolate and pastry shop;

Stella McCartney opening boutiques in the Palais Royal; further east, rue Étienne-Marcel is good for youth-oriented labels, while rue Vieille-du-Temple in the Marais is a must-see for its chic mix of small boutiques and intriguing concept stores.

Out of the Rain
In the Sentier and Opéra districts, explore delightful, shop-lined 19th-century arcades, full of quirky and interesting small boutiques that make them an excellent place to linger if the weather is poor.

Buy the Best
Seek out great French flair and quality, not just in fashion but also high-quality cookware—Le Creuset saucepans, Sabatier knives, kitchen gadgets that actually work, such as a Peugeot peppermill, a fine piece of kitchen engineering—and in stylish children's and baby clothes. For epicurean delights try exquisite prepared foods from Fauchon (▷ 126) or La Grande Épicerie at Le Bon Marché, handmade chocolates and fine wines, which all make tempting buys.

Down to Earth
If luxury and high fashion are not for you there are bargains to be had, so join the locals at the legendary flea markets, starting with Marché aux Puces de Saint-Ouen (▷ 26–27).

WHAT'S WHAT
Boulangeries sell baguettes, and more besides; try the *ficelle*, a thinner, finer loaf, or *pain au levain*, delicious sourdough bread. And then there are the croissants, *ordinaire* or *au beurre* (with butter). *Pâtisseries* sell pastries and tarts. *Charcuteries* sell cold meats, snails, cheese, truffles, wines, caviar and more. *Parfumeries* can stock solely French perfume but some sell cosmetics and soaps, too. *Bouquinistes* sell used books and prints, posters and postcards.

the latest shoe trends from Rodolphe Menudier; Bleu d'Auvergne cheese for sale at Marché Président Wilson; shops on the place du Marché Saint-Honoré

Directory

Around the Tour Eiffel

Antiques
Galerie Captier
Department Stores
Le Bon Marché Rive Gauche
Home and Garden
The Conran Shop

Latin Quarter, St-Germain and Islands

Accessories/Shoes
Lollipops
Books and CDs
La Hune
Shakespeare and Company
Candles and Scents
Dyptique
Clothes and Hats
Marie Mercié
Sonia Rykiel
Zadig & Voltaire
Food and Drink
Pierre Hermé
Rue Mouffetard
Markets
Marché aux Fleurs
Posters
Galerie Documents

Marais and Bastille

Accessories/Shoes
Jean-Baptiste Rautureau
Art
Artazart
Clothes and Hats
Agnès B
Antik Batik
Azzedine Alaïa
Coton Doux
L'Eclaireur
Free'P'Star
Surface 2 Air
Vanessa Bruno
Department Stores
BHV
Malls
Forum des Halles

Food and Drink
Mariage Frères
Home and Garden
Dehillerin
La Droguerie
Markets
Marché de la rue Montorgueil

Louvre and Champs-Élysées

Accessories/Shoes
Cartier
Christian Louboutin
Louis Vuitton
Antiques
Louvre des Antiquaires
M. G. Segas
Beauty
Detaille
Books and CDs
Galerie de l'Opéra de Paris
Clothes and Hats
Chanel
Colette
Didier Ludot
Dior
The Kooples
Department Stores
Galeries Lafayette (▷ panel, 126)
Printemps (▷ panel, 126)
Food and Drink
À la Mère de Famille
Fauchon
Toys
Si Tu Veux

Montmartre

Books and CDs
Librairie des Abbesses
Clothes and Hats
Judith Lacroix
Petit Bateau
Food and Drink
Boulangerie Delmontel
Markets
Marché Barbès
Marché de la rue Lepic

Shopping A-Z

À LA MÈRE DE FAMILLE

www.lameredefamille.com

This original 18th-century grocery shop has shelves laden with imaginatively created chocolates, jams and unusual groceries.

🔲 H2 ✉ 33–35 rue du Faubourg Montmartre, 75009 ☎ 01 47 70 83 69 🕐 Mon–Sat 9.30–8, Sun 10–1 🚇 Le Peletier, Cadet

AGNÈS B

europe.agnesb.com

Agnès B's fashion is the epitome of young Parisian chic; sharply cut clothes with original details.

🔲 J4 ✉ 6 rue du Jour, 75001 ☎ 01 45 08 56 56 🕐 Mon–Sat 10–7.30 🚇 Les Halles

ANTIK BATIK

www.antikbatik.fr

This is the place to shop for ethnic-chic fashions, including blouses, batik-printed stoles and lingerie.

🔲 L6 ✉ 18 rue de Turenne, 75004 ☎ 01 44 78 02 00 🕐 Mon 12.30–7.30, Tue–Sat 10.30–7.30, Sun 1.30–7.30 🚇 Saint-Paul

ARTAZART

www.artazart.com

Located on the banks of the Canal Saint-Martin, this bookshop specializes in design, architecture, photography and fashion. A small gallery shows work by up-and-coming artists.

🔲 M7 ✉ 83 quai de Valmy, 75010 ☎ 01 40 40 24 00 🕐 Mon–Fri 10.30–7.30, Sat 11–7.30, Sun 1–7.30 🚇 Jacques Bonsergent, République

AZZEDINE ALAÏA

The place to come for silhouette-hugging dresses by an artistic genius of the fashion world.

🔲 K6 ✉ 7 rue de Moussy, 75004 ☎ 01 42 72 19 19 🕐 Mon–Sat 10–7 🚇 Hôtel de Ville

BHV

www.bhv.fr

You can't buy shoes in this department store, but otherwise it's famous for having everything you'll ever need, from baby clothes to an electrical transformer.

🔲 K6 ✉ 55 rue de la Verrerie, 75004 ☎ 01 42 74 90 00 🕐 Mon–Tue, Thu–Fri 9.30–7.30, Wed 9.30–9, Sat 9.30–8 🚇 Hôtel de Ville

LE BON MARCHÉ RIVE GAUCHE

www.lebonmarche.com

You'll find the classiest goods in this Left Bank store. The modernist interior adds to the elegant atmosphere. Don't miss the beauty shop on the ground floor and the food hall, La Grande Épicerie, in an adjoining building, stocking delicacies from all over the world.

🔲 F7 ✉ 24 rue de Sèvres, 75007 ☎ 01 44 39 80 00 🕐 Mon–Wed, Sat 10–8, Thu–Fri 10–9 🚇 Sèvres-Babylone

BOULANGERIE DELMONTEL

www.arnaud-delmontel.com

This bakery and pastry shop stands out on a street known for its many mouthwatering food shops.

FASHION HUBS

Most of the big-name designers are on rue du Faubourg Saint-Honoré and avenue Montaigne, but you'll also find women's high fashion on the place des Victoires (home to Kenzo and Victoire), the rue Étienne-Marcel and towards Les Halles. The Marais's offerings run between rue de Sévigné, rue des Rosiers, place des Vosges and side streets. In Saint-Germain, look along and off boulevard Saint-Germain, on rue de Grenelle and up boulevard Raspail.

Arnaud Delmontel won the city of Paris's prize for best baguette in 2007 and became official supplier to the presidential residence.
🔛 C3 ✉ 39 rue des Martyrs, 75009 ☎ 01 48 78 29 33 🕔 Mon, Wed–Sat 7am–8.30pm, Sun 7–2.30 🚇 Notre-Dame-de-Lorette

CARTIER

www.cartier.fr

This is the traditional Paris home of the exclusive jeweller, known the world over, selling contemporary and vintage jewellery, watches, leather goods and perfumes. There's another branch right around the corner on place Vendôme.
🔛 G3 ✉ 13 rue de la Paix, 75002 ☎ 01 58 18 23 00 🕔 Mon–Sat 10.30–7 🚇 Opéra

CHANEL

www.chanel.com

Classy yet sexy, Chanel's fashion embodies Parisian elegance. At this main store there is everything from fashion to jewellery, leather goods, watches, sunglasses, perfume and beauty products.
🔛 D4 ✉ 42 avenue Montaigne, 75008 ☎ 800 25 50 05 🕔 Mon–Sat 10–7 🚇 Franklin D Roosevelt

CHRISTIAN LOUBOUTIN

www.christianlouboutin.com

A shoe fetishist's dream, Christian Louboutin is the place to go for exquisite women's shoes with glamour, extreme heels and the distinctive red soles.
🔛 H5 ✉ 19 rue Jean-Jacques Rousseau 75001 ☎ 01 42 36 53 66 🕔 Mon–Sat 10.30–7 🚇 Louvre-Rivoli

COLETTE

www.colette.fr

The place to go for leading design in fashion and home furnishings.
🔛 G4 ✉ 213 rue Saint-Honoré, 75001 ☎ 01 55 35 33 90 🕔 Mon–Sat 11–7 🚇 Tuileries, Pyramides

THE CONRAN SHOP

www.conranshop.fr

English designer Sir Terence Conran is a hit with the Parisian crowd. Fine materials, a post-1970s influence and sometimes an ethnic twist give Conran's furniture a modern elegance. Bathroom, kitchen and garden accessories complete the range. A small selection of fine foods from all over the world is also sold in this superb building, designed by Gustave Eiffel.
🔛 F7 ✉ 117 rue du Bac, 75007 ☎ 01 42 84 10 01 🕔 Mon–Fri 10–7, Sat 10–7.30 🚇 Sèvres-Babylone

COTON DOUX

www.cotondoux.com

You'll find pure cotton men's shirts at this kaleidoscope of colours and patterns, plus boxer shorts, silk ties, scarves and pyjamas.

K6 ✉ 24 rue de la Verrerie, 75002
☎ 01 44 54 09 29 ◷ Mon–Sat 10–8, Sun
11–8 Ⓜ Hôtel de Ville

DEHILLERIN
www.e-dehillerin.fr
Come here for all your kitchen
needs—copper pans, knives, bains-
marie, sieves and more. A
mail-order service is also available.
H4 ✉ 18–20 rue Coquillière, 75001
☎ 01 42 36 53 13 ◷ Mon 9–12.30, 2–6,
Tue–Sat 9–6 Ⓜ Les Halles, Louvre-Rivoli

DETAILLE
www.detaille.com
This Paris beauty shop, which celebrated its centenary in 2005, was
opened by the Countess de Presle,
one of the first people in Paris to
own a car and inventor of the
store's best-selling antipollution
face cream, Baume Automobile.
G2 ✉ 10 rue Saint-Lazare, 75009
☎ 01 48 78 68 50 ◷ Tue–Sat 11–1, 2–7
Ⓜ Notre-Dame-de-Lorette

DIDIER LUDOT
www.didierludot.fr
Rare vintage designer clothes
(Chanel, Dior, Balmain, Givenchy,
Lanvin) and classic Hermès handbags are sold at this shop in a
picturesque location.
H4 ✉ 20–24 Galerie Montpensier,
75001 ☎ 01 42 96 06 56 ◷ Mon–Sat
10.30–7 Ⓜ Palais-Royal– Musée du Louvre

DIOR
www.dior.com
Dior's historic headquarters sells
everything from the ready-to-wear
collection to menswear, jewellery
and accessories.
C4 ✉ 30 avenue Montaigne, 75008
☎ 01 40 73 73 73 ◷ Mon–Sat 10–7
Ⓜ Franklin D Roosevelt

DYPTIQUE
www.dyptiqueparis.com
Dyptique sells the ultimate in beautifully crafted candles, in a choice of
48 exquisite scents. There's also a
divine range of eaux de cologne.
J7 ✉ 34 boulevard Saint-Germain,
75005 ☎ 01 43 26 77 44 ◷ Mon–Sat
10–7 Ⓜ Maubert-Mutualité

LA DROGUERIE
www.ladroguerie.com
This gem of a store sells everything
you'll need to make your own
jewellery, knit for all the family or
customize accessories.
J4 ✉ 9 rue du Jour, 75001 ☎ 01 45
08 93 27 ◷ Mon 2–6.45, Tue–Sat 10.30–
6.45 Ⓜ Les Halles

L'ECLAIREUR
www.leclaireur.com
Planks, recycled materials and
video screens create a fantasy
world at this extraordinary Marais
fashion store, which stocks cutting-
edge designer labels. There's a
men's store around the corner in
rue Malher in a glass-roofed
former artist's studio.

Vintage fashion at Didier Ludot

➕ L6 ✉ 40 rue de Sévigné, 75003 ☎ 01 48 87 10 22 🕐 Mon–Sat 11–7 🚇 Saint-Paul, Chemin Vert

FAUCHON
www.fauchon.com
Paris's most renowned *épicerie* is a visual and gastronomic feast for foodies, complete with pâtisserie, deli and wine shop in imposing premises close to the Madeleine.
➕ F3 ✉ 24–26 place de la Madeleine, 75008 ☎ 01 42 96 06 56 🕐 Mon–Sat 9–8.30 🚇 Madeleine

FORUM DES HALLES
www.forumdeshalles.com
This partly-underground shopping complex is the biggest in central Paris and contains a few surprises —including a Muji store—among its predominantly mainstream fashion offerings. The complex will be radically redesigned in the next few years to address the short-comings of its 1980s design.
➕ J5 ✉ 1–7 rue Pierre-Lescot, 75001 🕐 Mon–Sat 10–8 🚇 Châtelet-Les Halles

DEPARTMENT STORES
Printemps and Galeries Lafayette, in the prestigious boulevard Haussmann, each stock hundreds of brands—from fashion to designer homeware. Printemps (🕐 Mon–Wed, Fri–Sat 9.35–7, Thu 9.35am–10pm 🚇 Havre-Caumartin) claims to have Europe's largest beauty department. Don't miss the art nouveau stained-glass cupola on the sixth floor of Printemps de la Mode, or the view from the ninth floor of Printemps de la Maison. At Galeries Lafayette (🕐 Mon–Sat 9.30–8; Thu until 9 🚇 Chaussée d'Antin) high-lights include the 1912 Byzantine-style glass dome and the Lafayette Gourmet food hall.

FREE'P'STAR
www.freepstar.com
There's a wonderful rummage sale ambience at this trendy second-hand clothes shop in the Marais, where the styles range from leopardskin to military surplus.
➕ K6 ✉ 81 rue de la Verrerie, 75004 ☎ 01 42 78 00 76 🕐 Mon–Sat 11–9, Sun 2–9 🚇 Hôtel de Ville

GALERIE CAPTIER
The antique Chinese and Japanese furniture (17th to 19th century) and old Japanese screens here have been chosen by owners Bernard and Sylvie Captier, who regularly travel to Asia to search out exotic and refined works of art.
➕ G6 ✉ 33 rue de Beaune, 75007 ☎ 01 42 61 00 57 🕐 Mon 2.30–7, Tue–Sat 10.30–7 🚇 Rue du Bac

GALERIE DOCUMENTS
For gifts, buy original posters and etchings from 1890 to 1940 by such masters as Toulouse-Lautrec and Alphonse Mucha.
➕ H6 ✉ 53 rue de Seine, 75006 ☎ 01 43 54 50 68 🕐 Tue–Sat 10.30–7, Mon 2.30–7 🚇 Odéon, Mabillon

GALERIE DE L'OPÉRA DE PARIS
This new boutique-bookshop focuses on opera and choreo-graphy, with all the latest CDs and books, as well as postcards, posters and presents.
➕ G3 ✉ Opéra Palais Garnier, rue Halévy, 75009 ☎ No phone 🕐 Daily 10–6.30 🚇 Opéra

LA HUNE
This excellent literary bookshop has an extensive art and architecture section. Open late.

G6 ✉ 170 boulevard Saint-Germain, 75006 ☎ 01 45 48 35 85 🕐 Mon–Sat 10am–11.45pm, Sun 11–7.45 🚇 Saint-Germain-des-Prés

JEAN-BAPTISTE RAUTUREAU

www.jeanbaptisterautureau.fr

Come here for your elegant formal men's shoes, with everything from black oxfords to chukka, Chelsea and biker boots, plus leather accessories.

K6 ✉ 16 rue du Bourg Tibourg, 75004 ☎ 01 42 77 01 55 🕐 Mon–Wed 11–1, 2–7.30, Sat 11–7.30, Sun 2–8 🚇 Saint-Paul, Hôtel de Ville

JUDITH LACROIX

www.judithlacroix.com

This high-end, very chic children's clothing store has some nice styles for *maman*, too.

b3 ✉ 3 rue Henry Monnier, 75009 ☎ 01 48 78 22 37 🕐 Mon–Sat 10–7 🚇 Saint-Georges

THE KOOPLES

www.thekooples.com

The Kooples sells sharp-looking, slim-fitting his-and-her fashions for youthful hipsters at accessible prices; a big hit in Paris and is now spreading internationally.

G4 ✉ 191 rue Saint-Honoré, 75001 ☎ 01 49 26 05 35 🕐 Mon 11–7, Tue–Fri 10.30–7.30, Sat 10.30–8 🚇 Louvre-Rivoli

LIBRAIRIE DES ABBESSES

A great little bookshop for those who read French or want to practise. Also has beautiful art books.

c2 ✉ 30 rue Yvonne le Tac, 75018 ☎ 01 46 06 84 30 🕐 Mon 11–8, Tue–Fri 9.30–8, Sat 10–8, Sun 12–8 🚇 Abbesses

LOLLIPOPS

www.lollipops.fr

A boho-chic collection of bags,

Louis Vuitton on the Champs-Élysées

scarves, hats and jewellery. The products are displayed by colour, making it particularly easy to find coordinating pieces.

L6 ✉ 2 rue des Rosiers, 75004 ☎ 01 42 77 43 75 🕐 Mon–Sat 10.30–7, Sun 11–7 🚇 Saint-Paul

LOUIS VUITTON

www.louisvuitton.com

The ultimate brand name's store on the Champs-Élysées was conceived as a continuation of a promenade on the avenue.

C3 ✉ 101 avenue des Champs-Élysées, 75008 ☎ 01 53 57 52 00 🕐 Mon–Sat 10–8, Sun 11–7 🚇 George V

LOUVRE DES ANTIQUAIRES

www.louvre-antiquaires.com

A huge, modernized complex of antiques shops where you'll find everything from Eastern carpets to furniture, silver, porcelain and paintings. The quality is good but expect high prices.

H5 ✉ 2 place du Palais-Royal, 75001 ☎ 01 42 97 27 27 🕐 Tue–Sun 11–7 (closed Sun in Jul and Aug) 🚇 Palais-Royal–Musée du Louvre

SHOP

Flower market on the Île de la Cité

MARCHÉ BARBÈS
Come to this colourful market for ethnic wares, scarves, fruit, vegetables and spices. Shop where the locals shop for a taste of Parisian neighbourhood banter.
🔢 Off map at d2 ✉ Boulevard de la Chapelle, 75018 🕒 Wed 7–2.30, Sat 7–3 🚇 Barbès-Rochechouart

MARCHÉ AUX FLEURS
This flower and plant market has everything you can imagine. Thousands of pots are displayed, plus trees and shrubs.
🔢 J6 ✉ Place Louis Lépine, 75004, Île de la Cité 🕒 Mon–Sat 8–7.30 (bird market on Sun) 🚇 Cité

MARCHÉ DE LA RUE LEPIC
It's up a steep hill but worth the effort to explore this atmospheric street, made famous in the film *Amélie* (2001). The best food shops are from the junction with rue des Abbesses down to boulevard de Clichy.
🔢 b2 ✉ Rue Lepic and rue des Abbesses, 75018 🕒 Most shops open Tue–Sat 9–1, 4–7, Sun 9–1 🚇 Abbesses, Blanche

MARCHÉ DE LA RUE MONTORGUEIL
Trendy bars and lunch places line this marble-paved pedestrian street.
🔢 J4 ✉ Rue Montorgueil, 75001 🕒 Food shops Tue–Sat 9–1, 4–7, Sun 9–1 🚇 Les Halles

MARIAGE FRÈRES
www.mariagefreres.com
This tea house, founded in 1854, offers hundreds of teas from all over the world, including some exclusive house blends.
🔢 K6 ✉ 30 rue du Bourg-Tibourg, 75004 ☎ 01 42 72 28 11 🕒 Daily 10.30–7.30; tea room 12–7 🚇 Hôtel de Ville

MARIE MERCIÉ
www.mariemercie.com
See extravagant hats for women here, from classic to theatrical. The men's store, Anthony Peto, is at 56 rue Tiquetonne, 75002.
🔢 H7 ✉ 23 rue Saint-Sulpice, 75006 ☎ 01 43 26 45 83 🕒 Mon–Sat 11–7 🚇 Odéon

M. G. SEGAS
This quirky but atmospheric vendor of antique walking canes is tucked into one of Paris's historic 19th-century shopping arcades.
🔢 H3 ✉ 34 passage Jouffroy, 75001 ☎ 01 47 70 89 65 🕒 Tue–Sat 12–6.30 or by appointment 🚇 Grands Boulevards

PETIT BATEAU
www.petit-bateau.com
Known for the excellent quality, every grown-up Parisienne has a Petit Bateau T-shirt—considered the best-fitting and most chic.
🔢 b2 ✉ 50 rue des Abbesses, 75018 ☎ 01 42 52 81 76 🕒 Mon–Sat 10–7 🚇 Abbesses

PIERRE HERMÉ

www.pierreherme.com

Pierre Hermé's couture pastries are as visually stunning as they are mouthwatering. His gold-leaf ornamented chocolate cake is legendary.

🗺 G7 ✉ 72 rue Bonaparte, 75006 ☎ 01 43 54 47 77 🕐 Sun–Wed 10–7, Thu–Fri 10–7.30, Sat 10–8 🚇 Saint-Sulpice, Mabillon

RUE MOUFFETARD

Visit this tourist classic straggling down a narrow, hilly street, for a wonderful array of shops and stalls selling fruit and veg, *charcuterie* and aromatic cheeses. Good café stops en route.

🗺 J9 ✉ Rue Mouffetard, 75005 🕐 Daily 🚇 Monge

SHAKESPEARE AND COMPANY

www.shakespeareandcompany.com

This charming English bookshop stocks new and used books. There is also a small library upstairs.

🗺 J7 ✉ 37 rue de la Bûcherie, 75005 ☎ 01 43 25 40 93 🕐 Mon–Fri 10am–11pm, Sat 11–11 🚇 Saint-Michel

SI TU VEUX

www.situveuxjouer.com

Si Tu Veux is the perfect toy shop with affordable toys, games and dressing-up gear. There's a separate section devoted to teddy bears.

🗺 H4 ✉ 68 Galerie Vivienne, 75002 ☎ 01 42 60 59 97 🕐 Tue–Sat 10.30–7 🚇 Bourse

SONIA RYKIEL

www.soniarykiel.com

In business since 1968, this ready-to-wear fashion house has ranges of accessories and perfumes.

🗺 G6 ✉ 175 boulevard Saint-Germain, 75006 ☎ 01 49 54 60 60 🕐 Mon–Sat 10.30–7 🚇 Saint-Germain-des-Prés

SURFACE 2 AIR

www.surfacetoair.com

This hip Marais 'concept' store sells contemporary men's and women's clothing influenced by everything from rock music and the military to Buñuel's *'Belle de Jour'*.

🗺 L5 ✉ 108 rue Vieille-du-Temple, 75003 ☎ 01 44 61 76 27 🕐 Mon–Sat 11.30–7.30, Sun 1.20–7.30 🚇 Saint-Paul, Filles du Calvaire

VANESSA BRUNO

www.vanessabruno.com

This designer's practical, easy-to-wear women's clothing with flair has won her a loyal following.

🗺 L5 ✉ 100 rue Vieille-du-Temple, 75003 ☎ 01 42 77 19 41 🕐 Mon 12.30–7.30, Tue–Sat 10.30–7.30, Sun 2–7 🚇 Filles du Calvaire

ZADIG & VOLTAIRE

www.zadig-et-voltaire.com

There's a trendy, youthful edge to the men's and womenswear at this Left Bank outpost of the internationally successful fashion house.

🗺 G6 ✉ 200 boulevard Saint-Germain, 75005 ☎ 01 45 49 10 34 🕐 Mon–Sat 10.30–7 🚇 Saint-Germain-des-Prés

SHOP

BOUTIQUING

The streets around the Abbesses Métro station offer a treasure trove of quirky independent clothing, accessories and gift boutiques. For fabulous food shops head down the rue des Abbesses and turn left on rue Lepic. Another wonderful food shopping area in Montmartre is the stretch of rue des Martyrs that descends below the boulevard de Clichy.

Entertainment

Once you've done with sightseeing for the day, you'll find lots of other great things to do with your time in this chapter, even if all you want to do is relax with a drink. In this section establishments are listed alphabetically.

ENTERTAINMENT

Introduction

The heart of Paris has a special beauty at night, and an electric atmosphere. Boulevards, great monuments and historic buildings are dazzlingly illuminated. The Champs-Élysées, place de la Concorde and the Louvre make a magnificent spectacle of lights against the night sky. The soaring Eiffel Tower, shining like gold and glittering for five minutes every hour, and the silvery white of the Sacré-Cœur Basilica are majestic landmarks.

Nightlife by Area

In a city as big as Paris there is no single focus for nightlife, and where you go will depend a lot on what you are looking for. Small theatres and jazz clubs still dot the Left Bank, with more of the latter around Châtelet and Les Halles, while there's often a chic and expensive feel to the bars and clubs in the west, between Étoile and Opéra. Fringing Montmartre, Pigalle and Clichy offer nightlife of an altogether more raffish kind, with sex shops and strip joints interspersed with mainstream discos and some of the city's best live music venues, so that despite the overt sleaze it's not an area to be written off lightly. The eastern *arrondissements* have some of the most interesting and fashionable nightlife, from the Marais's gay scene and *branché*

AN EVENING STROLL

Start at Châtelet and walk towards the Louvre along the embankment opposite the illuminated Conciergerie, the Monnaie and the Institut de France. At the Louvre make a detour into the magnificently lit Cour Carrée. Return to the river, cross the Pont des Arts, then walk back along the opposite bank, with views north of the stately Samaritaine and the Palais de Justice on the Île de la Cité. Continue towards Saint-Michel, then cross over to Notre-Dame and make your way around the north side of the island, which offers good views.

Clockwise from top: Evening view of the domed Institut de France with the Pont des Arts in the foreground; the Publicis Drugstore in the Champs-Élysées; cafés, bars

ENTERTAINMENT

(hippest) café society to the scuffed boho chic of lively rue Oberkampf.

Glamorous Fun

There's a sense of excitement, anticipation and enjoyment. In addition to glamorous cabarets, there are world-class ballet, concert and opera venues, nightclubs, discos, café-theatres and atmospheric bars with live music. Although the Métro is closed from 1.15am (2.15 Friday and Saturday) to 5.30am, many taxis run at night, as well as the Noctilien buses (www.noctilien.fr).

Clubbing Paris Style

Dressing up—not down—is still often the rule when you go dancing in Paris, and if your clothes don't pass muster you may not get past the door at the more chic nightclubs. Drinks prices can be steep but the price of entry often includes a *conso* (free drink).

Added Magic

A boat trip along the Seine between the illuminated buildings adds extra magic and *bateaux mouches* run every evening until 10.30 (9 in winter). For experienced in-line skaters a high-speed three-hour skating tour of Paris takes place every Friday at 9.30pm (see www.pari-roller.com for details).

GAY PARIS

As befits a city which has had an openly gay mayor—Bertrand Delanoë—for the last decade, Paris is a welcoming place for lesbian and gay visitors, particularly in the fashionable Marais district, where the list of gay-friendly or mixed venues stretches beyond the established confines of the 'official' gay scene. The hugely popular Open Café (✉ 17 rue des Archives ☎ 01 48 8780 25; www.opencafe.fr) and slick, trendy Raidd (✉ 23 rue du Temple ☎ 01 42 77 04 88) are two of the area's best places to see and be seen in.

and clubs line the streets of Montmartre; the Reservoir Club; out on the town, a delightful evening scene in Paris; Le Showcase nightclub; the famous Moulin Rouge

Directory

Around the Tour Eiffel

Cinemas
La Pagode
Clubs
Petit Journal Montparnasse

Latin Quarter, St-Germain and Islands

Bars
Caveau de la Huchette
Cinemas
Le Champo
Lucernaire/Centre National
 d'Art et d'Essai
Studio Galande
Classical Music
Musée National du Moyen-Âge
Clubs
Jane Club
Theatres
Théâtre de la Huchette
Théâtre de Nesle

Marais and Bastille

Cinemas
Forum des Images
Clubs
Duc des Lombards
Favela Chic
Sunset-Sunside
Contemporary Music/Dance
Café de la Danse
Opera
Opéra Bastille
Sport
Piscine des Halles
 (Suzanne Berlioux)
Theatre/Dance
Théâtre du Châtelet
Théâtre de la Ville

Louvre and Champs-Élysées

Bars
Barramundi
Harry's New York Bar
Cinemas
Le Balzac
Classical Music
Auditorium du Louvre
Clubs
Le Baron
Club l'Arc
Queen
Shows
La Belle Époque
Theatres
Comédie Française/Salle Richelieu

Montmartre

Bars
La Fourmi
Cinemas
Studio 28
Clubs
Folie's Pigalle
Michou
Contemporary Music
La Boule Noire/La Cigale
Divan du Monde
L'Élysée-Montmartre
Shows
Moulin Rouge
Theatres
Bouffes du Nord

Entertainment A-Z

AUDITORIUM DU LOUVRE

www.louvre.fr

A high-quality series of lunchtime and evening concerts are held in this 450-seat auditorium beneath the Louvre's pyramid.

🞤 G5 ✉ Musée du Louvre (entrance by the pyramid), 75001 ☎ 01 40 20 55 55 🚇 Palais-Royal

LE BALZAC

www.cinemabalzac.com

Le Balzac is famous for its screenings of American independent films (in the original language) and for the debates that often follow. Concerts are held before Saturday evening screenings. Bar on site.

🞤 B3 ✉ 1 rue Balzac, 75008 ☎ 01 45 61 10 60 🚇 George V, Charles de Gaulle–Étoile

LE BARON

www.clublebaron.com

Once a high-class hostess club and now a hot nightspot that attracts stars and VIPs, Le Baron was founded by trendy graffiti artist André and features top DJs.

🞤 B4 ✉ 6 avenue Marceau, 75008 ☎ 01 47 20 04 01 🕐 Daily 11pm–dawn 🚇 Alma-Marceau, Étoile

BARRAMUNDI

www.barramundi.fr

Barramundi draws a fashionable crowd with its world music, bar, lounge and eclectic restaurant.

🞤 H3 ✉ 3 rue Taitbout, 75009 ☎ 01 47 70 21 21 🕐 Mon–Fri 12–3.30pm, 6.30pm–2am, Sat 7pm–5am 🚇 Richelieu-Drouot, Chaussée d'Antin

LA BELLE ÉPOQUE

www.belleepoqueparis.com

The truly sparkling show 'La Vie est Belle' (Life is Beautiful) includes the cancan, which the audience is

then invited to dance. Fine French cuisine is served during the show.

🞤 G4 ✉ 36 rue des Petits-Champs, 75002 ☎ 01 42 96 33 33 🕐 Show: daily 6pm and 9pm 🚇 Pyramides

BOUFFES DU NORD

www.bouffesdunord.com

Many plays here, staged by director Peter Brook, are not only excellent but also in English.

🞤 Off map at d2 ✉ 37 bis boulevard de la Chapelle, 75010 ☎ 01 46 07 34 50 🚇 La Chapelle

LA BOULE NOIRE/LA CIGALE

www.lacigale.fr

Famous names have played at the diminutive La Boule Noire, in the heart of Pigalle, including Franz Ferdinand, Jamie Cullum and Metallica. It's linked to a former theatre, La Cigale, a listed historic monument, and hosts musicals, rock and pop, and music festivals.

🞤 c2 ✉ 120 boulevard Rochechouart, 75018 ☎ 01 49 25 81 75 🚇 Pigalle, Anvers

CAFÉ DE LA DANSE

www.cafedeladanse.com

Pop, rock and world music in an auditorium that feels homey,

Numerous classical music concerts are held in churches—try Saint-Eustache, Saint-Germain-des-Prés, Saint-Julien-le-Pauvre, Saint-Louis-en-l'Île, Saint-Roch and Saint-Séverin (www.ampconcerts.com). Seats are reasonably priced and the quality of music is sometimes very high. May to September free concerts are held in parks. Schedules are available at the Office du Tourisme or the Hôtel de Ville.

despite seating more than 300. Also some theatre and dance.
⊞ Off map ✉ 5 passage Louis-Philipe, 75011 ☎ 01 47 00 57 59 🚇 Bastille

CAVEAU DE LA HUCHETTE
www.caveaudelahuchette.fr
Still going strong after 60 years having regularly hosted all the great names in jazz, this atmospheric basement bar with dancing and live jazz starts bopping from 9.30pm onwards.
⊞ J7 ✉ 5 rue de la Huchette, 75005 ☎ 01 43 26 65 05 🚇 Saint-Michel

LE CHAMPO
www.lechampo.com
Come here for cult classics; retrospectives explore the work of directors such as the Marx Brothers, Claude Chabrol and Jacques Tati. Films are in the original language.
⊞ J7 ✉ 51 rue des Écoles, 75015 ☎ 01 43 54 51 60 🕑 Daily, times vary 🚇 Saint-Michel, Odéon, Cluny-La Sorbonne

CLUB L'ARC
www.larc-paris.com
This restaurant/club opposite the Arc de Triomphe is ideal for sipping cocktails from the huge, covered terrace. The ambience is chic, vintage and intimate.
⊞ B2 ✉ 12 rue de Presbourg, 75016 ☎ 01 45 00 78 70 🕑 Restaurant Mon–Fri lunch, dinner, Sat dinner. Club Thu, Fri, Sat from 11.30pm 🚇 Charles de Gaulle–Étoile

COMÉDIE FRANÇAISE/SALLE RICHELIEU
www.comedie-francaise.fr
The Comédie Française, home to France's most prestigious troupe of actors, was founded by Louis XIV in 1680. Today, the repertoire is made up of the classics, including works by Shakespeare, Molière, and a few modern pieces.
⊞ G4 ✉ 1 place Colette, 75001 ☎ 08 25 10 16 80 🕑 Performances daily times vary, some matinées Sat, Sun 🚇 Palais-Royal–Musée du Louvre

DIVAN DU MONDE
www.divandumonde.com
The lower level of this former brothel is devoted to concerts of everything from rock to electronic and world music; the Divan Japonais upstairs holds themed evenings with DJs and video artists showing their talents.
⊞ c3 ✉ 75 rue des Martyrs, 75018 ☎ 01 40 05 06 99 🚇 Pigalle

DUC DES LOMBARDS
www.ducdeslombards.com
Prestigious jazz musicians regularly play in this Les Halles club.
⊞ J5 ✉ 42 rue des Lombards, 75001 ☎ 01 42 33 22 88 🕑 Closed Sun 🚇 Châtelet

L'ÉLYSÉE-MONTMARTRE
www.elyseemontmartre.com
This concert venue is in a building designed by Gustave Eiffel with

ENTERTAINMENT

mostly new rock groups. Also a club with regular theme evenings: rock, reggae or drum and bass.

➕ C2 ✉ 72 boulevard Rochechouart, 75018 ☎ 01 44 92 45 47 🕐 Mon–Thu noon–2am, Fri–Sat noon–3am 🚇 Anvers

FAVELA CHIC

www.favelachic.com

The sounds, flavours and vibrant style of urban Brazil ring out in a grungy but trendy setting, with a restaurant, live bands and DJs.

➕ M3 ✉ 18 rue du Faubourg du Temple, 75011 ☎ 01 40 21 31 14 🕐 Tue–Sat 7.30pm–late 🚇 Pigalle

FOLIE'S PIGALLE

This small club was once an Italian-style theatre, then a strip club. It has a different theme every evening and a Brazilian tea dance on Sunday evening.

➕ b2 ✉ 11 place Pigalle, 75009 ☎ 01 48 78 55 25 🕐 Mon–Sat 11pm–dawn, Sun from 8pm 🚇 Pigalle

FORUM DES IMAGES

www.forumdesimages.fr

Films or documentaries shot in or connected with Paris and film classics are screened here. A cheap day pass admits you to all the day's screenings. See website for films in other venues.

➕ J5 ✉ 2 rue du Cinéma, Port Saint-Eustache, Forum des Halles, 75001 ☎ 01 44 76 63 00 🕐 Mon–Fri 12.30pm–9pm, Sat 2pm–9pm 🚇 Les Halles, Châtelet

LA FOURMI

This is a great bar with a retro feel and a funky bottle-rack chandelier, drawing a young hip crowd.

➕ C2 ✉ 74 rue des Martyrs, 75018 ☎ 01 42 64 70 35 🕐 Mon–Thu 8am–2am, Fri–Sat 8am–4am, Sun 10am–2am 🚇 Pigalle

HARRY'S NEW YORK BAR

www.harrys-bar.fr

Harry's in New York was dismantled and shipped lock, stock and barrel just before World War I. It's popular with the British and French and offers hundreds of cocktails.

➕ G3 ✉ 5 rue Daunou, 75002 ☎ 01 42 61 71 14 🕐 Sun–Thu noon–2am, Fri–Sat noon–3am 🚇 Opéra

JANE CLUB

www.janeclub.fr

The brand new Jane Club is an intimate space with room for up to 250 people, offering both DJ nights and live shows. Check the website to find out what's on—the mix includes eclectic with electro-swing, 80s nights, disco and funk.

➕ H7 ✉ 62 rue Mazarine, 75006 ☎ 01 55 42 22 01 🕐 Usually open Fri–Sun, times vary 🚇 Saint-Germain-des-Prés, Odéon

LUCERNAIRE/CENTRE NATIONAL D'ART ET D'ESSAI

www.lucernaire.fr

This complex of three cinemas, an art gallery, bar, restaurant and three theatres stages a wide variety of plays. Housed in a former factory, it attracts top French actors.

POOLS AND HORSES

Paris's municipal swimming pools have complicated opening hours largely geared to schoolchildren. Phone to check for public hours and avoid Wednesday and Saturday, both popular with children off school. If horse-racing is your passion, don't miss the harness-racing at Vincennes (www.hippodrome-vincennes.com), with its brilliant flashes of colour-coordinated horses and jockeys. Check the racing newspaper *Paris-Turf* for race schedules.

🔲 G8 ✉ 53 rue Notre-Dame-des-Champs, 75006 ☎ 01 45 44 57 34 🚇 Vavin, Notre-Dame-des-Champs

MICHOU
www.michou.fr
A familiar sight in the district, Michou is always dressed in electric-blue suits and big eyeglasses. The drag show in this venerable club is still going strong.
🔲 c2 ✉ 80 rue des Martyrs, 75018 ☎ 01 46 06 16 04 🕐 Nightly dinner 8.30, show 10.45 🚇 Pigalle

MOULIN ROUGE
www.moulinrouge.fr
The 'Red Windmill', made famous by Toulouse-Lautrec, is the birthplace of the saucy cancan. The Moulin Rouge is expensive; expect to pay €99 for the cheapest show without drinks or a meal.
🔲 b2 ✉ 82 boulevard de Clichy, 75018 ☎ 01 53 09 82 82 🕐 Nightly dinner and show 7pm; show only 9 and 11 🚇 Blanche

MUSÉE NATIONAL DU MOYEN-ÂGE
www.musee-moyenage.fr
This medieval mansion is home to a museum (▷ 34–35), but it also hosts classical and chamber music concerts.

🔲 J7 ✉ 6 place Paul-Painlevé, 75005 ☎ 01 53 73 78 16 🕐 Wed–Mon 9.15–5.45; free concerts of medieval music: times vary 🚇 Cluny–La Sorbonne

OPÉRA BASTILLE
www.operadeparis.fr
Paris's 'people's' opera house towers over place de la Bastille and boasts five moveable stages, which make it a technological feat in itself. The range of performances include opera, operettas, recitals, ballet, dance and even theatre.
🔲 M7 ✉ 120 rue de Lyon, 75012 ☎ 08 92 89 90 90 🚇 Bastille

LA PAGODE
This film theatre inside an oriental pagoda shows cult classics and modern films in their original language. There's an adjoining Japanese garden and tea room.
🔲 E7 ✉ 57 bis rue de Babylone, 75007 ☎ 01 45 55 48 48 🕐 Varies 🚇 Saint-François Xavier

PETIT JOURNAL MONTPARNASSE
www.petitjournalmontparnasse.com
This club, sister venue to the Petit Journal Saint-Michel, has hosted some of France's best-loved jazz musicians, and you can dine while listening or just have a drink.
🔲 E9 ✉ 13 rue Commandant-Mouchotte, 75014 ☎ 01 43 21 56 70 🕐 Closed Sun and 3 weeks in summer 🚇 Montparnasse-Bienvenüe

PISCINE DES HALLES (SUZANNE BERLIOUX)
Fully renovated, this underground 50m (164ft) pool is overlooked by lush tropical gardens.
🔲 J5 ✉ Forum des Halles, Niveau–3, 75001 ☎ 01 42 36 98 44 🚇 Les Halles

QUEEN

www.queen.fr

This large club is still going strong and is popular with both straights and gays. Top DJs, with different themes each evening.

C3 102 avenue des Champs-Élysées, 75008 0892 70 73 30 Daily midnight–7am (times can vary, some nights start earlier) George V

STUDIO 28

www.cinemastudio28.com

The coolest cinema in Paris, where new releases in the original language change every day or two; has its own little bar and garden.

b2 10 rue Tholozé, 75018 01 46 06 36 07 Abbesses, Blanche

STUDIO GALANDE

www.studiogalande.fr

Cult movie *The Rocky Horror Picture Show* is shown here every Friday and Saturday at 10.10pm. The rest of the week screenings vary from art films to cartoons.

J7 42 rue Galande, 75005 01 43 26 94 08 Saint-Michel, Maubert-Mutualité, Cluny

SUNSET-SUNSIDE

www.sunset-sunside.com

Two jazz clubs: the Sunset offers electric jazz and world music concerts, while the Sunside concentrates on acoustic jazz.

J5 60 rue des Lombards, 75001 01 40 26 21 25 Châtelet

THÉÂTRE DU CHÂTELET

www.chatelet-theatre.com

The Théâtre du Châtelet hosts a varied schedule of opera, symphonic music and dance, as well as popular Sunday morning concerts. It seats 2,500 people.

J6 Place du Châtelet, 75001 01 40 28 28 40 Châtelet

SO MUCH CHOICE

Paris has a huge number of wonderful bars and wine bars to choose from. These range from bars selling just beer, to cocktail and late-night bars dotted throughout the city. Most Parisian wine bars are small, neighbourly places, some selling food as well. You will find a great selection of regional wines. Explore the various areas to find a plethora of convivial drinking holes.

THÉÂTRE DE LA HUCHETTE

www.theatre-huchette.com

Two of Ionesco's masterpieces, *La Cantatrice Chauve* (The Bald Soprano) and *La Leçon* (The Lesson), have been performed here six days a week for over 50 years. Room for just 85 people.

J7 23 rue de la Huchette, 75005 01 43 26 38 99 Saint-Michel

THÉÂTRE DE NESLE

www.theatredenesle.com

This small Left Bank theatre is in the vaulted basement of a 17th-century mansion. Occasional English-language plays and regular shows for kids (in French).

H6 8 rue de Nesle, 75006 01 46 34 61 04 Odéon, Pont Neuf

THÉÂTRE DE LA VILLE

www.theatredelaville-paris.com

This modern venue showcases an adventurous agenda of avant-garde music, contemporary dance and plays, which include works by Shakespeare and Marlowe.

J6 2 place du Châtelet, 75004 01 42 74 22 77 Performances: times vary Châtelet

Eat

There are places to eat across the city to suit all tastes and budgets. In this section establishments are listed alphabetically.

EAT

Introduction

Paris is often described as the capital of gastronomy, so a meal out in the city has a lot to live up to. The standard for the best restaurants—the Michelin star—is famed throughout the world as the epitome of gastronomic excellence.

Budget Choices
If your budget isn't up to the crème-de-la-crème, there are hundreds of less expensive choices, from regional French cuisine to North African, Lebanese or Japanese.

The Very Best
Restaurants have higher prices than brasseries or bistros but will often provide a refined setting, elegant cuisine and a good wine list. For a special treat, look for multi-starred Michelin chefs such as Alain Ducasse and Guy Savoy. Dress smartly and book in advance.

Lunch and Snacks
Cafés and bars serve coffee, tea, soft drinks, alcohol and snacks. Most open from around 9am (or earlier) until well into the evening and many have outdoor seating. *Salons de thé* (tea rooms) open from noon until evening. If you are on a budget, have your main meal at lunchtime, when most restaurants serve a reasonably priced *menu du jour*, or daily menu, of two or three courses with a glass of wine.

OPENING TIMES

Most restaurants and bistros keep strict serving times. Restaurants open at 12, close at 2.30, then reopen at 7.30 or 8. Most Parisians take an hour for lunch and eat in the staff canteen or in a local bistro. The evening meal is the most important of the day and is usually taken *en famille* between 8 and 9pm. Restaurants stop taking orders between 10 and 11pm. To eat later, try the Les Halles area or a brasserie. Some restaurants close on weekends and in July and August, and some shut for holidays in February.

From top: L'Espadon dining room at the Paris Ritz; coffee at Le Petit Fer à Cheval in the Marais; menu at Guy Savoy; artistry meets cuisine

EAT

Directory

Around the Tour Eiffel

Asian
Benkay
French-Bistro
L'Affriolé
Le Cristal de Sel
L'Entêtée
French-Brasserie
Brasserie Thoumieux
French-Elegant
Le Ciel de Paris
Le Clarisse
Le Jules Verne
French-Regional
L'Ami Jean

Latin Quarter, St-Germain and Islands

Asian
Yugaraj
French-Bistro
Le Comptoir
Louis Vins
Le Petit Saint-Benoît
French-Brasserie
La Coupole
Le Petit Zinc
French-Elegant
La Tour d'Argent
Trendy
Alcazar
Ze Kitchen Galerie

Marais and Bastille

French-Bistro
Au Pied de Cochon
Bistrot L'Oulette
La Muse Vin
Pramil
French-Brasserie
Bofinger
La Tête Ailleurs
French-Elegant
Le Dôme du Marais
French-Regional
Benoit

Kosher
L'As du Fallafel
North African
404
Trendy
Georges
Monjul

Louvre and Champs-Élysées

French-Bistro
Café Marly
Jean
French-Elegant
Le Céladon
Guy Savoy
Passage 53
Taillevent
French-Regional
Carré des Feuillants
Fusion
6 New York
Spoon
Trendy
Le Senderens

Montmartre

French-Bistro
Au Virage Lepic
Café Burq
Le Progrès
French-Regional
Au Clair de la Lune
Trendy
Rose Bakery

Further Afield

French-Bistro
La Petite Ardoise
French-Brasserie
Chalet des Îles
French-Elegant
Gordon Ramsay au Trianon
La Grande Cascade
Trendy
Le Styx

EAT

Eating A-Z

PRICES

Prices are approximate, based on a 3-course meal for one person.

€€€	over €90
€€	€30–€90
€	under €30

404 €€

For a different taste, this fashionable Moroccan restaurant serves up excellent North African cuisine.

🔛 K4 ✉ 69 rue des Gravilliers, 75003 ☎ 01 42 74 57 81 🕐 Daily lunch, dinner 🚇 Arts et Métiers

6 NEW YORK €€

www.6newyork.fr

6 New York offers beautiful contemporary decor and fusion food.

🔛 B5 ✉ 6 avenue de New York, 75016 ☎ 01 40 70 03 30 🕐 Mon–Fri lunch, dinner, Sat dinner 🚇 Alma-Marceau

L'AFFRIOLÉ €€

This popular 'nouveau bistro' is great value for the money; friendly service and classic French dishes with a twist (such as pig's-feet croquettes or pork ribs in red wine).

🔛 C5 ✉ 17 rue Malar, 75007 ☎ 01 44 18 31 33 🕐 Tue–Sat lunch, dinner 🚇 Pont de l'Alma, Invalides

ALCAZAR €€

www.alcazar.fr

English designer Terence Conran's bar-cum-restaurant offers some of the best fish in town. The lounge bar upstairs has international DJs.

🔛 H6 ✉ 62 rue Mazarine, 75006 ☎ 01 53 10 19 99 🕐 Daily lunch, dinner 🚇 Odéon

L'AMI JEAN €€

www.amijean.eu

This unassuming, friendly restaurant specializes in Basque dishes. Veal, beef and seafood are enhanced by fine wines.

🔛 C5 ✉ 27 rue Malar, 75007 ☎ 01 47 05 86 89 🕐 Daily lunch, dinner 🚇 Pont de l'Alma, La Tour Maubourg

L'AS DU FALLAFEL €

This cheap-and-cheerful kosher restaurant has a cult following among visitors and Marais trendies

Coffees and beers in the Marais district

alike for its delicious falafel and low prices. An advantage here is that you can choose to eat in or take away.

⊞ L6 ✉ 34 rue des Rosiers, 75007 ☎ 01 48 87 63 60 🕐 Sun–Thu 12–12, Fri lunch only 🚇 Saint-Paul

AU CLAIR DE LA LUNE €€

Classically French cuisine is served in this comfortable, welcoming inn-style restaurant just off the place du Tertre. It's run by two brothers and is very popular with locals. Warm ambience without being too touristy.

⊞ c1 ✉ 9 rue Poulbot, 75018 ☎ 01 42 58 97 03 🕐 Daily lunch, dinner 🚇 Abbesses

AU PIED DE COCHON €€

www.pieddecochon.com

Pigs' trotters feature at this Parisian institution, but there are other delicious offerings, such as seafood and sublime French onion soup, served in elegant surroundings.

⊞ J4 ✉ 6 rue Coquillère, 75001 ☎ 01 40 13 77 00 🕐 Daily 24 hours 🚇 Les Halles

AU VIRAGE LEPIC €–€€

This welcoming bistro, in the heart of Montmartre, is well-known for its tasty meat-based main courses and delicious puddings, complemented by a great wine list. In summer you can sit outside.

⊞ b1 ✉ 61 rue Lepic, 75018 ☎ 01 42 52 46 79 🕐 Wed–Mon 7pm–11.30pm 🚇 Blanche, Abbesses

BENKAY €€

Dine here on modern Japanese food with panoramic views from the fourth floor of the Novotel Paris Tour Eiffel. Good *teppanyaki*.

⊞ A7 ✉ 61 quai de Grenelle, 75015 ☎ 01 40 58 21 26 🕐 Daily lunch, dinner 🚇 Bir-Hakeim

BENOIT €€–€€€

www.benoit-paris.com

This long-standing Michelin-starred bistro serving classic regional dishes is owned by chef Alain Ducasse. Reserve ahead.

⊞ J6 ✉ 20 rue Saint-Martin, 75004 ☎ 01 42 72 25 76 🕐 Daily lunch, dinner 🚇 Hôtel de Ville, Châtelet-Les Halles

BISTROT L'OULETTE €€

www.l-oulette.com

This tiny bistro homes in on Gascony, *cassoulet* and duck.

⊞ M6 ✉ 38 rue des Tournelles, 75004 ☎ 01 42 71 43 33 🕐 Mon–Fri lunch, dinner, Sat dinner 🚇 Bastille

BOFINGER €€

www.bofingerparis.com

Claiming to be the oldest brasserie in Paris (1864), Bofinger serves seafood, *choucroute* and steaks.

⊞ M6 ✉ 5 rue de la Bastille, 75004 ☎ 01 42 72 87 82 🕐 Daily lunch, dinner 🚇 Bastille

BRASSERIE THOUMIEUX €€

www.thoumieux.fr

This brasserie was established in 1923. The elegant dining room

EAT

FRENCH MEAN CUISINE

'The only cooks in the civilized world are French. Other races have different interpretations of food. Only the French understand cuisine because their qualities—rapidity, decision-making, tact—are used. Who has ever seen a foreigner succeed in making a white sauce?' —Nestor Roqueplan (1804–70), Editor of *Le Figaro*.

LA COUPOLE

Horror struck Parisian hearts in the mid-1980s when it was announced that La Coupole had been bought by property developers and several floors were to be added on top. This happened, but the famous old murals (by Juan Gris, Soutine, Chagall, Delaunay and many more) have been reinstated, the red-velvet seats preserved and the art deco lights duly restored. The 1920s interior is now a historic monument.

has velvet wall seats and lots of mirrors. Expect hearty meals such as *cassoulet* (sausage and bean casserole) or duck dishes, including foie gras. The two-star Michelin Restaurant Jean-François Piège occupies the first floor, but you will need plenty of cash to experience its culinary creations.

🖽 D5 ⊠ 79 rue Saint-Dominique, 75007 ☎ 01 47 05 49 75 🕐 Daily 12–12 🚇 Invalides

CAFÉ BURQ €€

The crowd is young and the decor minimalist in this tiny Montmartre bistro, with a bar on one level and the dining room a few steps down. The food and wine are delicious and the service is pleasant.

🖽 b2 ⊠ 6 rue Burq, 75018 ☎ 01 42 52 81 27 🕐 Mon–Sat dinner only 🚇 Abbesses

CAFÉ MARLY €€

www.beaumarly.com

This classy café-restaurant located in the Louvre itself must have the best terrace in the world, with its exceptional view of I. M. Pei's glass pyramid and the opposite wing of the museum behind it. The food is reliably good, the service

is friendly and the interior is elegantly decorated.

🖽 G5 ⊠ 93 rue de Rivoli, 75001 ☎ 01 49 26 06 60 🕐 Daily 8am–2am 🚇 Palais-Royal–Musée du Louvre

CARRÉ DES FEUILLANTS €€€

www.carredesfeuillants.fr

You'll find an elegant setting for Alain Dutournier's brilliant evocation of the cooking of his native Gascony. He uses the best ingredients to wonderful effect, earning two Michelin stars.

🖽 F4 ⊠ 14 rue de Castiglione, 75001 ☎ 01 42 86 82 82 🕐 Mon–Fri lunch, dinner, Sat dinner. Closed Aug 🚇 Tuileries

LE CÉLADON €€–€€€

Interesting variations on French classics, and at weekends it opens as Le Petit Céladon.

🖽 G3 ⊠ Hotel Westminster, 15 rue Daunou, 75002 ☎ 01 47 03 40 42 🕐 Mon–Fri lunch, dinner. Closed Aug 🚇 Opéra

CHALET DES ÎLES €€

www.chalet-des-iles.com

The only way to get to this big chalet-style restaurant (seats 100), on an island on one of the Bois de Boulogne lakes, is by a small ferry-boat. Enjoy traditional French food. A fireplace and piano player in winter create a warm ambience.

⊠ Bois de Boulogne Lac Inférieur, 75016 ☎ 01 42 88 04 69 🕐 Apr–Oct daily lunch, dinner; Nov–Mar Tue–Sat lunch, dinner, Sun lunch 🚇 Rue de la Pompe

LE CIEL DE PARIS €€–€€€

www.cieldeparis.com

Whizz your way up to the 56th floor of the Tour Montparnasse, to the highest restaurant in Paris. The changing menu may include pan-

The French are famous for their crusty bread

sautéed fillet of beef with a truffle sauce, lobster risotto, or fried scallops with a parsley purée.

🔛 F9 ✉ Tour Montparnasse, 33 avenue du Maine, 75015 ☎ 01 40 64 77 64 🕐 Daily lunch, dinner 🚇 Montparnasse-Bienvenüe

LE CLARISSE €€

www.leclarisse.fr
Understated black-and-white design sets the scene for Japanese chef Sadaki Kajiwara's innovative cooking, which combines French tradition with Asian touches and plenty of fish and seafood.

🔛 D5 ✉ 29 rue Surcouf, 75007 ☎ 01 45 50 11 10 🕐 Tue–Fri lunch, Mon–Sat dinner 🚇 Invalides

LE COMPTOIR €€

This gastro-bistro, under the expert eye of chef Yves Camdeborde, champions modern French cuisine. Reservations are not taken for lunch, but it's best to reserve ahead for dinner.

🔛 H7 ✉ Hôtel Relais Saint-Germain, 9 carrefour de l'Odéon, 75006 ☎ 01 43 29 12 05 🕐 Daily lunch, dinner 🚇 Odéon

LA COUPOLE €€

www.lacoupole-paris.com
The most historic of Montparnasse's brasseries offers reasonably-priced set menus but the elegant art deco setting and buzzy ambience are what make it memorable.

🔛 F9 ✉ 102 boulevard du Montparnasse, 75014 ☎ 01 43 20 14 20 🕐 Daily lunch, dinner 🚇 Vavin

LE CRISTAL DE SEL €€

www.lecristaldesel.fr
Watch chef Karil Lopez in his tiny kitchen as he turns out simple, satisfying food using the freshest seasonal produce in this very popular restaurant.

🔲 Off map ✉ 13 rue Mademoiselle,
75015 ☎ 01 42 50 35 29 🕒 Tue–Sat
lunch, dinner 🚇 Commerce

🔲 Off map ✉ 4 rue Danville, 75014
☎ 01 40 47 56 81 🕒 Tue–Fri lunch,
dinner, Sat dinner 🚇 Denfert Rochereau

LE DÔME DU MARAIS €€

www.ledomedumarais.fr
Seasonal produce meets creative
modern touches in dishes like *tom
yam* (Thai soup) of wild sea bream
at this discreet restaurant in the
domed rotunda of a former chapel.
🔲 L5 ✉ 53 bis rue des Francs-Bourgeois,
75004 ☎ 01 42 74 54 17 🕒 Tue–Sat
lunch, dinner 🚇 Hôtel de Ville, Rambuteau,
Saint-Paul

L'ENTÊTÉE €€

This restaurant has changed hands
but still turns out excellent French
dishes with just the right hint of
Asian taste in a tiny space with
simple, modern decor.

Go to Guy Savoy for delectable oysters

GEORGES €€

On the top floor of the Pompidou
Centre (▷ 16–17), the inventive
modern cuisine at Georges is
complemented by a stunning view
over Paris.
🔲 K5 ✉ 19 rue Beaubourg, 75004 ☎ 01
44 78 47 99 🕒 Wed–Mon lunch, dinner
🚇 Rambuteau

GORDON RAMSAY AU TRIANON €€€

www.gordonramsay.com
Round off a day of splendour in
Versailles with a sumptuous dinner
in Gordon Ramsay's much-praised
dining room in the Trianon Palace
Hotel, where the menu makes lavish use of luxurious ingredients
such as lobster and foie gras. It
holds two Michelin stars.
🔲 Off map ✉ 1 boulevard de la Reine,
78000, Versailles ☎ 01 30 84 55 55
🕒 Tue–Sat dinner only 🚆 SNCF Versailles
Rive Droite or RER Versailles Rive Gauche

LA GRANDE CASCADE €€€

www.grandecascade.com
Napoleon III built this pavilion at
the foot of La Grande Cascade
(the Great Waterfall) for his visits
to the Bois de Boulogne. It
became a restaurant in 1900. The
windows in the circular dining
room give magical views of the

NEW BISTROS

Paris may be the food capital of the world, with more than its share of top restaurants, but
not everyone can afford the astronomical prices of the best eateries. Some 15 years ago a
few famous chefs opened 'baby bistros', which benefited from their expertise but offered
fine meals in often nondescript surroundings for reasonable prices. The trend has now
expanded and Paris is full of 'nouveaux bistros'.

EAT

woods. The Michelin-starred chef, Frédéric Robert, creates fine French cuisine.

✉ Allée de Longchamp, Bois de Boulogne, 75016 ☎ 01 45 27 33 51 🕐 Daily lunch, dinner 🚇 Porte Maillot, then bus 244

GUY SAVOY €€€

www.guysavoy.com

At this gastronomic temple Guy Savoy makes cooking an art form. Expensive, of course, but certainly exquisite. The restaurant has three Michelin stars.

🔲 B2 ✉ 18 rue Troyon, 75017 ☎ 01 43 80 40 61 🕐 Tue–Fri lunch, dinner, Sat dinner 🚇 Charles de Gaulle–Étoile

JEAN €€–€€€

www.restaurantjean.fr

Solid comfort, one Michelin star and creative dishes like roast pigeon with aubergine caviar are followed by desserts with names like Oh, Canada or French Twist.

🔲 H2 ✉ 8 rue Saint-Lazare, 75009 ☎ 01 48 78 62 73 🕐 Mon–Fri lunch and dinner. Closed Aug 🚇 Notre-Dame-de-Lorette, Trinité

LE JULES VERNE €€€

www.lejulesverne-paris.com

Alain Ducasse's Michelin-starred restaurant, located on level two of the Eiffel Tower, is the talk of Paris. It has spectacular views over the city and is popular and very expensive. Reservations are essential.

🔲 B6 ✉ 2nd level, Tour Eiffel, 75007 (private elevator) ☎ 01 45 55 61 44 🕐 Daily lunch, dinner 🚇 Bir-Hakeim

LOUIS VINS €€

This large restaurant with a quirky and lively ambience is excellent value. No credit cards.

LOCAL WINE

At the intersection of rue Saule and rue Saint-Vincent there is a small hillside of vines—a remnant of the former vineyards of the Butte Montmartre. During the wine harvest there is a very popular, colourful festival with plenty of tastings. For more information visit www.fetedesvendanges demontmartre.com.

🔲 J7 ✉ 9 rue de la Montaigne-Sainte-Geneviève, 75005 ☎ 01 43 29 12 12 🕐 Daily lunch, dinner 🚇 Maubert-Mutualité

MONJUL €€

www.monjul.com

Talented chef Julien Agobert produces inventive dishes that are a work of art, and taste as good as they look.

🔲 K5 ✉ 28 rue des Blancs Manteaux, 75004 ☎ 01 42 74 40 15 🕐 Tue–Sat lunch, dinner 🚇 Rambuteau

LA MUSE VIN €€

This bistro and wine bar specializes in wines at low prices, with a good selection of delicious, generous fresh food.

🔲 Off map ✉ 101 rue Charonne, 75011 ☎ 01 40 09 93 05 🕐 Mon–Fri lunch, dinner, Sat dinner 🚇 Charonne

PASSAGE 53 €€–€€€

www.passage53.com

Shinishi Sato's tiny restaurant in Paris's oldest shopping arcade packs a culinary punch, combining wonderful French ingredients with an inventive modern approach. Sato is the first Japanese chef in France to earn two Michelin stars. Reservation is recommended.

🔲 H3 ✉ 53 Passage des Panoramas, 75002 ☎ 01 42 33 04 35 🕐 Tue–Sat lunch, dinner 🚇 Grands Boulevards

EAT

Taillevent is renowned for good food

LE PETIT SAINT-BENOÎT €
www.petit-st-benoit.com
This popular, inexpensive old classic was once the haunt of writers; the decor has barely changed since the 1930s.
🔲 G6 ✉ 4 rue Saint-Benoît, 75006 ☎ 01 42 60 27 92 🕐 Tue–Sat lunch, dinner 🚇 Saint-Germain-des-Prés

LE PETIT ZINC €€
www.petit-zinc.com
There's a classic Belle Époque interior in this brasserie, which serves inspiring dishes such as cod and chorizo or mouth-watering Grand Marnier soufflé.
🔲 G6 ✉ 11 rue Saint-Benoît, 75006 ☎ 01 42 86 61 00 🕐 Daily noon–midnight 🚇 Saint-Germain-des-Prés

LA PETITE ARDOISE €€
www.restaurantpetiteardoise.fr
Regarded as one of the most popular restaurants in Fontainebleau, La Petite Ardoise serves classic French dishes.
🔲 Off map ✉ 16 rue Montebello, 77300 Fontainebleau ☎ 01 64 24 08 66 🕐 Tue–Fri lunch, dinner 🚇 Fontainebleau-Avon

PRAMIL €€
www.pramilrestaurant.fr
You can't go wrong with the refined food and reasonable prices in this small, chic restaurant.
🔲 L4 ✉ 9 rue du Vertbois ☎ 01 42 72 03 60 🕐 Tue– Sat lunch, dinner, Sun dinner 🚇 Arts et Métiers, Temple

LE PROGRÈS €–€€
This is the kind of café where you'd expect to see a character from *Amélie*, which was filmed in the area. Animated staff and *plat du jour* at lunchtime.
🔲 c2 ✉ 7 rue des Trois-Frères, 75018 ☎ 01 42 64 07 37 🕐 Daily 9am–2am 🚇 Abbesses

ROSE BAKERY €–€€
Organic food is served in this trendy English bakery and tea shop owned by a Franco-British couple. Popular for Sunday brunch.
🔲 c3 ✉ 46 rue des Martyrs, 75009 ☎ 01 42 82 12 80 🕐 Tue–Fri 9–4, Sat, Sun 10–4 🚇 Pigalle, Notre-Dame-de-Lorette

LE SENDERENS €€€
www.senderens.fr
Tired of all the fuss of owning a Michelin three-star restaurant, Alain Senderens closed down Lucas Carton and opened the simpler and somewhat less expensive Le Senderens. Michelin has awarded the restaurant two stars.
🔲 F3 ✉ 9 place de la Madeleine, 75008 ☎ 01 42 65 22 90 🕐 Daily lunch, dinner (closed 2–24 Aug) 🚇 Madeleine

SPOON €€€
www.spoon.tm.fr
Chef Alain Ducasse's highly original 'world food' menu lets you mix and match at his trendy bistro-style restaurant with open kitchen.

➕ C4 ✉ 12 rue de Marignan, 75008
☎ 01 40 76 34 44 🕓 Mon–Fri lunch,
dinner. Closed Aug, 25 Dec–3 Jan
🚇 Franklin D. Roosevelt

LE STYX €

Decorated with mismatched furniture and junkshop finds as decor, this amiable little restaurant-cum-bar is typical of rue Oberkampf's boho charms, but is a little less frantic than some. Food is eclectic—*feijoada* (bean and meat stew) followed by apple crumble perhaps—and there's a mellow soundtrack of jazz and flamenco.

➕ Off map ✉ 126 rue Oberkampf, 75011
☎ 01 48 05 92 88 🕓 Daily lunch, dinner
🚇 Ménilmontant, Parmentier

TAILLEVENT €€€

www.taillevent.com
The cooking has classical foundations with subtle modern leanings at this discreetly elegant restaurant. Opened in 1950, it steadily gained its reputation and is the worthy possessor of two Michelin stars.

➕ C2 ✉ 15 rue Lamennais, 75008 ☎ 01
44 95 15 01 🕓 Mon–Fri lunch, dinner.
Closed Aug 🚇 George V, Charles de Gaulle–Étoile

LA TÊTE AILLEURS €€

www.lateteailleurs.fr
This spacious yet warm Mediterranean-inspired place has chandeliers, stone walls, wall hangings and comfy seating.

➕ L7 ✉ 20 rue Beautreillis, 75004 ☎ 01
42 72 47 80 🕓 Tue–Fri lunch, dinner, Mon, Sat dinner 🚇 Saint-Paul, Bastille

LA TOUR D'ARGENT €€€

www.latourdargent.com
Come to this historic restaurant in the Latin Quarter for its fabulous view, its great wine cellar and the tasty duck. It may have been demoted to one Michelin star, but it is still superb.

➕ K7 ✉ 15–17 quai de la Tournelle, 75005 (facing Île Saint-Louis) ☎ 01 43 54 23 31 🕓 Tue–Sat lunch, dinner 🚇 Pont-Marie, Cardinal Lemoine

YUGARAJ €€

www.restaurant-indien-yugaraj.fr
One of the best Indian restaurants in Paris, with beautiful decor and attentive service, Yugaraj serves discreet traditional curries, plus surprising dishes and tasty tandooris.

➕ H6 ✉ 14 rue Dauphine, 75006 ☎ 01
43 26 44 91 🕓 Tue, Wed, Fri–Sun lunch, dinner, Thu dinner 🚇 Pont Neuf, Odéon

ZE KITCHEN GALERIE €€

www.zekitchengalerie.fr
Inventive cuisine shines out at this chic restaurant with an elegant modern interior. A typical menu could be a starter of marinated octopus with lemongrass, a main of duck with foie gras and plums, and to finish, a pudding such as strawberry and rhubarb sorbet.

➕ H6 ✉ 4 rue des Grands-Augustins, 75006 ☎ 01 44 32 00 32 🕓 Mon–Fri lunch, dinner, Sat dinner 🚇 Odéon

EAT

PICNIC LUNCHES

If your taste is for a *déjeuner sur l'herbe* in Fontainebleau, the rue Grande grocery shops are perfect for picnic supplies. In Versailles, the Marché Notre-Dame is an excellent covered market (closed on Mondays) for stocking up on lunch items. When in Chantilly, allow yourself to be tempted by the patisseries, with their delicious cakes and pastries, with lashings of the eponymous cream.

Sleep

Ranging from luxurious and modern upmarket hotels to simple budget hotels, Paris has accommodation to suit everyone. In this section establishments are listed alphabetically.

SLEEP

Introduction

The city's hotels have had a (sometimes deserved) reputation for being dated and uncomfortably small, but recent years have seen a complete overhaul. Boutique hotels have sprung up all over the city, especially in the Marais. Hotels around the Louvre, Champs-Élysées and Opéra tend to be more expensive, while those in the Latin Quarter are often smaller and more affordable.

Finding a Good Deal
Some of the luxury hotels are out of another era. Their stated prices are high but discounts can be found online or through some travel agents. Paris is one of the rare European capitals where you can find a pleasant, affordable place to stay in a central part of the city. The Paris Tourist Office (▷ 166) has information. You can reserve rooms if you visit in person.

Helpful Tips
Prices often drop in July and August and rise in May, June, September and October, for the trade fairs. Check whether the price includes breakfast. If you are bringing or renting a car, ask whether parking is available and the cost.

Outer Limits
Chain hotels on the outskirts can be less expensive, but they lack character. You'll also have to spend more time taking the Métro.

APARTMENT LIVING

● To rent an apartment, options include the UK-based Apartment Service (tel 020 8944 1444 from the UK; 011 44 20 8944 1444 from the US; www.apartmentservice.com); Home Rental Service at 120 avenue des Champs-Élysées, 75008 (tel 01 42 25 65 40; www.homerental.fr); and Paris Lodging at 25 rue Lacépède, 75005 (tel 01 43 36 71 69; www.parislodging.fr).
● For bed-and-breakfast try France Lodge at 2 rue Meissonnier, 75017 (tel 01 56 33 85 80; www.francelodge.fr).

From top: Hôtel Plaza Athénée; the luxurious Salon Cambon at the Paris Ritz; revolving doors at the Hôtel de Crillon; the Bernstein suite at the Hôtel de Crillon

Directory

Around the Tour Eiffel
Budget
Hôtel de l'Avre

Latin Quarter, St-Germain and Islands
Budget
Hôtel du Collège de France
Timhotel Jardin des Plantes
Mid-Range
The Five Hotel
Hôtel de l'Abbaye
Hôtel d'Angleterre
Hôtel Atlantis Saint-Germain-des-Prés
Hôtel Design de la Sorbonne
Hôtel Duc de Saint-Simon
Hôtel Lenox
Hôtel des Marronniers
Hôtel La Perle
Hôtel Sainte-Beuve
Hôtel de l'Université
Les Rives de Notre-Dame
Luxury
L'Hôtel
Hôtel du Jeu de Paume
Hôtel Montalembert

Marais and Bastille
Budget
Grand Hôtel Malher
Hôtel de la Place des Vosges
Luxury
Murano Urban Resort
Pavillon de la Reine

Louvre and Champs-Élysées
Budget
Hôtel Chopin
Mid-Range
Hôtel Lautrec Opéra
Hôtel Molière
Hotel Résidence Foch
Résidence Lord Byron
Luxury
Hôtel de Crillon
Hôtel San Régis

Montmartre
Budget
Hôtel Prima Lepic
Timhotel Montmartre

SLEEP

Sleeping A-Z

PRICES
Prices are approximate and based on a double room for one night.

€€€	€251–€800
€€	€151–€250
€	€50–€150

THE FIVE HOTEL €€
www.thefivehotel.com
There are tiny rooms but plenty of designer punch in this hotel, on a quiet street in Montparnasse. The 23 bright rooms are scented with the heavenly fragrances of Diptyque and boast fun lighting effects and original artwork.
J9 ✉ 3 rue Flatters, 75005 ☎ 01 43 31 73 21 🚇 Gobelins

GRAND HÔTEL MALHER €
www.grandhotelmalher.com
This family hotel, with 28 well-equipped rooms, has an excellent location in the Marais district near the opera house.
L6 ✉ 5 rue Malher, 75004 ☎ 01 42 72 60 92 🚇 Saint-Paul

155

L'HÔTEL €€€

www.l-hotel.com

L'Hôtel is a Parisian legend that is exuberantly elegant and intimate. Oscar Wilde stayed here and celebrities are often to be found in the discreet bar. Restaurant and some superb rooms. 20 rooms.

➕ G6 ✉ 13 rue des Beaux-Arts, 75006 ☎ 01 44 41 99 00 🚇 Saint-Germain-des-Prés

HÔTEL DE L'ABBAYE €€–€€€

www.hotel-abbaye.com

This quaint, historic hotel was once a convent. The lounge and most of the 40 rooms look out onto a patio. Four duplex apartments, four junior suites.

➕ G7 ✉ 10 rue Cassette, 75006 ☎ 01 45 44 38 11 🚇 Saint-Sulpice

HÔTEL D'ANGLETERRE €€

www.hotel-dangleterre.com

This former 18th-century British embassy has a garden patio and 26 spacious rooms. Ernest Hemingway lived in room 14 in 1921. There is a bar and relaxing piano lounge.

➕ G6 ✉ 44 rue Jacob, 75006 ☎ 01 42 60 34 72 🚇 Saint-Germain-des-Prés

BUDGET HOTELS

Gone are the heady days when Paris was peppered with atmospheric basic hotels with their inimitable signs 'eau à tous les étages' (water on every floor). Now there are usually bath or shower rooms with every bedroom, resulting in higher prices and smaller rooms. So don't expect much space in budget hotel rooms and you may not get breakfast included; but receptionists usually speak a second language in hotels with two or more stars.

HÔTEL ATLANTIS SAINT-GERMAIN-DES-PRÉS €–€€

www.hotelatlantis-sg.com

Most of the 27 bright and airy rooms face onto pretty place Saint-Sulpice. All have been beautifully decorated with antiques and fine artwork, and have good facilities. The communal areas are elegant but welcoming.

➕ G7 ✉ 4 rue du Vieux-Colombier, 75006 ☎ 01 45 48 31 81 🚇 Saint-Sulpice

HÔTEL DE L'AVRE €

www.hoteldelavre.com

Minutes from the Eiffel Tower, this is an impeccably kept two-star hotel. Breakfast is served in the pretty garden in spring and summer. There are 25 rooms.

➕ B8 ✉ 21 rue de l'Avre, 75015 ☎ 01 45 75 31 03 🚇 La Motte-Picquet Grenelle

HÔTEL CHOPIN €

www.hotelchopin.fr

Tucked into a historic shopping arcade, this charming small hotel offers 36 simple en-suite rooms and a very warm welcome in an excellent location just minutes from the opera.

➕ J7 ✉ 46 passage Jouffroy, 75009 ☎ 01 47 70 58 10 🚇 Grands Boulevards

HÔTEL DU COLLÈGE DE FRANCE €

www.hotel-collegedefrance.com

This tranquil 29-room hotel is situated near the Sorbonne.

➕ J7 ✉ 7 rue Thénard, 75005 ☎ 01 43 26 78 36 🚇 Maubert–Mutualité

HÔTEL DE CRILLON €€€

www.crillon.com

This fabulous Parisian classic reeks of glamour, style and history, but is closed for refurbishment until 2015.

📍 E4 ✉ 10 place de la Concorde, 75008
☎ 01 44 71 15 00 🚇 Concorde

HÔTEL DESIGN DE LA SORBONNE €€

www.hotelsorbonne.com

This hotel has contemporary living down to a fine art. Each floor has photos, engravings and literary quotes that complement the British-style decor. The 38 bedrooms have iMac computers, among the opulent facilities.

📍 H8 ✉ 6 rue Victor-Cousin, 75005
☎ 01 43 54 58 08 🚇 Cluny–La Sorbonne

HÔTEL DUC DE SAINT-SIMON €€

www.hotelducdesaintsimon.com

Rather pricey (at the top end of mid-range) but the antiques and picturesque setting just off boulevard Saint-Germain justify it. 34 comfortable rooms, and an intimate atmosphere. Reserve far ahead.

📍 F6 ✉ 14 rue Saint-Simon, 75007
☎ 01 44 39 20 20 🚇 Rue du Bac

HÔTEL DU JEU DE PAUME €€€

www.jeudepaumehotel.com

A small, delightful hotel carved out of a 17th-century royal tennis court. 30 tasteful rooms with beams. There are some suites and two spacious apartments for longer stays.

📍 K7 ✉ 54 rue Saint-Louis-en-l'Île, 75004
☎ 01 43 26 14 18 🚇 Pont Marie

HÔTEL LAUTREC OPÉRA €–€€

www.paris-hotel-lautrec.com

This three-star hotel is named after the artist Henri Toulouse-Lautrec, who once lived here. It is classified as a historic monument and has a beautiful 18th-century facade.

Inside, there's a more contemporary feel, with pale wood furniture and blue-and-yellow upholstery. Some rooms have exposed bricks and beams but with 21st-century equipment such as satellite TV.

📍 H3 ✉ 8–10 rue d'Amboise, 75002
☎ 01 42 96 67 90 🚇 Richelieu-Drouot

HÔTEL LENOX €€

www.hotelparislenoxsaintgermain.com

Popular with the design and fashion world for its restored, stylish 1930s bar, Hôtel Lenox has 34 rooms, and T. S. Eliot's ghost.

📍 G6 ✉ 9 rue de l'Université, 75007
☎ 01 42 96 10 95 🚇 Saint-Germain-des-Prés

HÔTEL DES MARRONNIERS €€

www.hotel-marronniers.com

The oak-beamed rooms and vaulted cellars here are converted to lounges. Ask for a room overlooking the garden. 37 rooms.

📍 G6 ✉ 21 rue Jacob, 75006 ☎ 01 43 25 30 60 🚇 Saint-Germain-des-Prés

HÔTEL MOLIÈRE €€

www.hotel-moliere.fr

On a quiet street near the Louvre and Opéra, Hôtel Molière has 32 clean, reasonably priced rooms. There is no restaurant on site.

SLEEP

🏁 G4 ✉ 21 rue Molière, 75001 ☎ 01 42 96 22 01 🚇 Pyramides, Palais-Royal

HÔTEL MONTALEMBERT €€€

www.hotel-montalembert.fr

On the Left Bank, this fashionable hotel has a patio, bar and restaurant, plus chic design details and 56 well-appointed rooms and 7 suites.

🏁 F6 ✉ 3 rue de Montalembert, 75007 ☎ 01 45 49 68 68 🚇 Rue du Bac

HÔTEL LA PERLE €€

www.hotel-paris-laperle.com

This attractive, renovated 17th-century building on a quiet street near Saint-Germain has 38 rooms.

🏁 G7 ✉ 14 rue des Canettes, 75006 ☎ 01 43 29 10 10 🚇 Mabillon

HÔTEL DE LA PLACE DES VOSGES €

www.hotelplacedesvosges.com

Located down a quiet street, this lovely 17th-century town house offers basic comforts. 16 rooms.

🏁 M6 ✉ 12 rue de Birague, 75004 ☎ 01 42 72 60 46 🚇 Bastille, Saint-Paul

HÔTEL PRIMA LEPIC €

www.29lepic.fr

This three-star hotel is near Sacré-Cœur. The brightly painted

LE CRILLON

Whether you stay at the Ritz, the Crillon, the Meurice, the Bristol or the Georges V, they all have their tales to tell, but that of the Crillon (▷ 156) is perhaps the most momentous. This mansion managed to survive the Revolution despite having the guillotine on its doorstep. Mary Pickford and Douglas Fairbanks spent their honeymoon here. Closed till 2015.

bedrooms have been carefully furnished, and five have canopy beds. Each has a TV, hairdryer and modem connection.

🏁 b2 ✉ 29 rue Lepic, 75018 ☎ 01 46 06 44 64 🚇 Blanche, Abbesses

HOTEL RÉSIDENCE FOCH €€

www.foch-paris-hotel.com

This three-star hotel has elegantly furnished rooms filled with good quality furniture and traditional French touches. There's a bright bar on the ground floor and a private courtyard garden where you can relax over breakfast or a drink.

🏁 Off map at A3 ✉ 10 rue Marbeau, 75016 ☎ 01 45 00 46 50 🚇 Porte Dauphine

HÔTEL SAINTE-BEUVE €€

www.parishotelcharme.com

Between Montparnasse and the Luxembourg gardens, this exclusive hotel features period antiques and modern furnishings. 22 rooms.

🏁 G8 ✉ 9 rue Sainte-Beuve, 75006 ☎ 01 45 48 20 07 🚇 Notre-Dame-des-Champs

HÔTEL SAN RÉGIS €€€

www.hotel-sanregis.fr

Popular with showbiz folk, this elaborately decorated hotel has 32 rooms and 11 suites.

🏁 D4 ✉ 12 rue Jean-Goujon, 75008 ☎ 01 44 95 16 16 🚇 Franklin D. Roosevelt, Champs-Élysées–Clémenceau

HÔTEL DE L'UNIVERSITÉ €€

www.universitehotel.com

This Left Bank hotel par excellence has individually decorated rooms (27), some with (non-working) fireplaces, antique furnishings and exposed beams.

SLEEP

Mid-priced establishments are popular with business visitors, so it is virtually impossible to find rooms during trade-fair seasons such as May to early June and mid-September to October. In summer many offer discounts as their clientele shrinks. All rooms are equipped with TV, phone, private bath or shower rooms, minibar and most with hairdryer. Air-conditioning is not standard, but elevators are common.

➕ G6 ✉ 22 rue de l'Université, 75007
☎ 01 42 61 09 39 🚇 Rue du Bac

MURANO URBAN RESORT €€€

www.muranoresort.com

Sharp modern design, variable lighting effects and great attention to detail characterize this trendy hotel with a highly popular bar and new covered terrace. In an up-and-coming area near the place de la République. In-house restaurant. 43 rooms and 9 suites.

➕ M4 ✉ 13 boulevard du Temple, 75003
☎ 01 42 71 20 00 🚇 République, Filles du Calvaire

PAVILLON DE LA REINE €€€

www.pavillon-de-la-reine.com

Period decoration and lavish furnishings in this 17th-century building are enhanced by the lovely leafy garden. No restaurant. 54 rooms and suites.

➕ M6 ✉ 28 place des Vosges, 75003
☎ 01 40 29 19 19 🚇 Bastille

RÉSIDENCE LORD BYRON €€

www.hotel-lordbyron.fr

Just off the Champs-Élysées, this comfortable, classy 31-room hotel has a pleasant small interior garden in which to relax.

➕ C2 ✉ 5 rue Châteaubriand, 75008
☎ 01 43 59 89 98 🚇 Georges V

LES RIVES DE NOTRE-DAME €€

www.rivesdenotredame.com

Overlooking the banks of the Seine, this hotel has beamed ceilings, marble tiling, tapestries and fine wrought-iron furniture. 10 rooms.

➕ J7 ✉ 15 quai Saint-Michel, 75005
☎ 01 43 54 81 16 🚇 Saint-Michel

TIMHOTEL MONTMARTRE €–€€

www.timhotel.com

On the charming, tree-shaded place Émile Goudeau, this pleasant hotel has the rare advantage of panoramic views of Paris from some rooms on its upper floors.

➕ b2 ✉ 11 rue Ravignan, 75018 ☎ 01 42 55 74 79 🚇 Abbesses

TIMHOTEL JARDIN DES PLANTES €

www.timhotel.com

This pretty 33-room hotel overlooks the botanical gardens and the natural history museum. There is a fifth-floor roof terrace.

➕ K8 ✉ 5 rue Linné, 75005 ☎ 01 47 07 06 20 🚇 Jussieu

Paris is trying to increase its small stock of bed-and-breakfasts by encouraging residents to open up their homes to visitors and establishing standards for B&Bs. If you'd like to stay with a French host, the following organizations can help you: Alcôve & Agapes: www.bed-and-breakfast-in-paris.com; Association Française BAB France: www.bedbreak.com; Fleurs de Soleil: www.fleursdesoleil.fr.

SLEEP

Need to Know

**This section takes you through all the
practical aspects of your trip to make it run
more smoothly and to give you confidence
before you go and while you are there.**

NEED TO KNOW

Planning Ahead

WHEN TO GO

Spring is a popular time, with its lovely chestnut blossoms. The city reaches peak tourist capacity in hot, sunny July. However, with the Parisian exodus to the countryside in August the city is emptier than usual. Autumn is busy with trade fairs and rooms can be scarce and expensive.

TIME

Paris is one hour ahead of London, six hours ahead of New York and nine hours ahead of Los Angeles.

TEMPERATURE

JAN	FEB	MAR	APR	MAY	JUN	JUL	AUG	SEP	OCT	NOV	DEC
6°C	7°C	12°C	16°C	20°C	23°C	25°C	26°C	21°C	16°C	10°C	7°C
43°F	45°F	54°F	61°F	68°F	73°F	77°F	79°F	70°F	61°F	50°F	45°F

Spring (April, May) takes time to get going. Things don't usually warm up until mid-May.
Summer (June to August) can be glorious. Days are longest in June, with the most sunshine and a pleasant temperature. Hot and sunny in July, it is often hot, humid and stormy in August.
Autumn (September to November) has crisp days and usually clear skies.
Winter (December to March) is rarely below freezing but it rains frequently, sometimes with hail, in January and March.

WHAT'S ON

January/February *Chinese New Year:* In Chinatown, 13th *arrondissement.*
April/May *International Paris Fair:* Consumer heaven at Porte de Versailles; www.foire deparis.fr.
Paris marathon: Starts from the Champs-Élysées; www.parismarathon.com.
May *Labour Day* (1 May): Parades and symbolic lily-of-the-valley bouquets.
La Nuit des Musées: On one Saturday evening museums fling their doors open with music, drama and readings.
June *Paris Jazz Festival* (mid-Jun–Jul): Weekends at parc Floral de Paris.

Fête de la Musique (21 Jun): Music on the streets.
La Marche des Fiertés LGBT de Paris (Gay Pride) (Sat in late Jun): Popular procession, plus partying in the Marais district.
July *Bastille Day* (14 Jul): The most important French festival celebrates the 1789 storming of the Bastille. Fireworks and street dances on the evening of the 13th and a parade on the 14th on the Champs-Élysées.
July–August *Paris Quartier d'Été:* Outdoor perform-ances; www.quartierdete.com.
Paris Plage: A beach along the quays of the Seine on

the Right Bank.
September *Festival d'Automne à Paris* (mid-Sep to end Dec): Music, theatre and dance all over the city; www.festival-automne.com.
October *Foire Internationale d'Art Contemporain:* Paris's biggest modern art fair; www.fiacparis.com.
Nuit Blanche: For one night various cultural venues open all night, free of charge.
November *Beaujolais Nouveau* (third Thu in Nov): Drinking in all the city's bars.
December Paris International Boat Show.

PARIS ONLINE

www.new-paris-ile-de-france.co.uk
The website of the Paris Île de France regional tourist authority has a huge quantity and variety of information on Paris and the surrounding region, including entertainment and events, shopping, sport and leisure, children's Paris, accommodation and public transport. It now has a new site dedicated to English-language speakers.

www.parisinfo.com
The Paris Tourist Office online, with listings and practical information, sightseeing and links to other useful sites covering every aspect of leisure in the city. There's also online hotel booking.

www.parisfranceguide.com
This site, aimed at English-speakers, is about getting orientated in Paris and finding what you are looking for—a job or an apartment, a hotel or events information.

www.parisvoice.com
Click here and you'll feel like you're already in the city. Intended for English-speaking Parisians, it gives an insider's view of the city, with features, events information, restaurant reviews, classified ads, a Q&A column (dealing with some very serious issues) and more.

www.paris.fr
The official site of Paris's mayor and city council has information on museums, theatres, parks and sport, as well as a virtual tour of the Hôtel de Ville. There is also a wealth of civic news aimed at Paris residents.

www.parissi.com
Look up this website for Paris disco, dance and clubland news (French only).

www.paris-update.com
What's happening, updated weekly: art shows, films, restaurants, concerts.

PRIME TRAVEL SITES

www.parisdigest.com
Independent city guide showing you around the city and providing mainstream practical information. A good range of hotel, restaurant and shopping guides.

www.fodors.com
A complete travel-planning site. You can research prices and weather; book air tickets, cars and rooms; ask questions (and get answers) from fellow travellers; and find links to other sites.

INTERNET CAFÉS

Milk Opéra
🖶 G3 ✉ 28 rue du Quatre-Septembre, 75001 ☎ 01 40 06 00 70; www.milklub.com
🕙 Daily 24 hours 🚇 Opéra

Odéon Cyber Cube
🖶 H7 ✉ 5 rue Mignon, 75006 ☎ 01 53 10 30 50
🕙 Daily 10–10
🚇 Censier-Daubenton

PARIS WIFI

For those with laptops or mobile phones, there is access to wireless internet free in 260 parks, libraries and public buildings across Paris. Hotspots are shown with distinctive oval signs. You'll need to link to Orange's WiFi page, select your pass, create a password, fill a form and agree to terms. Each free session lasts up to two hours.

Getting There

GETTING YOUR BEARINGS

Think of Paris as a snail, with its shell curling around the 1st *arrondissement* (district) right in the middle. The numbers of the other *arrondissements* follow clockwise, ending with the 20th on the eastern side of the city. *C'est logique, non?*

AIRPORTS

Most international flights arrive at Roissy Charles de Gaulle airport, with some international and French domestic flights arriving at Orly airport. Paris has good rail connections, including the Eurostar train direct from London.

Roissy Charles de Gaulle Airport
Bus 45–60 min, €10
Train 35 min, €9.50

Orly Airport
Bus 30 min, €7.20
Train 35 min, €11.30

60km (40 miles)

FROM ROISSY CHARLES DE GAULLE

Roissy (tel 3950; outside France 331 70 36 39 50; www.adp.fr) is 23km (14 miles) northeast of central Paris and has three terminals. Air France currently operates out of Terminal 2. There are three ways to get to the city. By bus: Air France (www.cars-airfrance.com) operates a bus service (Line 4) between the airport and Montparnasse and Gare de Lyon, every 30 minutes 6am–10pm (€16.50), and to the Arc de Triomphe (Étoile) and Porte Maillot (Line 2) every 20–30 minutes, 6am–11pm (€15). You can buy tickets from the driver or at the Air France offices in the terminal. Or take the 50-minute trip on Roissybus that runs every 15 or 20 minutes from Terminals 1, 2 and 3 to Opéra 6am–11pm (€10). By train: A surburban train network, the RER (Réseau Express Régional) Line B takes around 35 minutes to central Paris (€9.50). Trains leave every 10–15 minutes. By taxi: A taxi costs around €50 (confirm the price with the driver before setting off) and takes between 30 minutes and 1 hour, depending on traffic. Allow for a 15 per cent increase in fares at night, on Sundays and public holidays.

FROM ORLY

Orly (tel 3950; outside France 331 70 36 39 50; www.adp.fr), the older and smaller of Paris's two main international airports, is 14km (8.5 miles) south of central Paris with no direct train to central Paris. By bus: Air France provides shuttle buses to Les Invalides and Gare Montparnasse every 20–30 minutes 5am–11.20pm (€11.50). The trip takes about 30 minutes. By train: The Orlyval train, which operates daily 6am–11pm, will take you to Antony, where you can change for line B of the main Paris RER rail system (€11.30). From here it's around 25 minutes to central Paris. By taxi: A taxi costs around €45 (confirm the price before setting off) and takes 15–30 minutes. Allow for a 15 per cent increase in fares at night, on Sundays and public holidays.

EUROSTAR

The Eurostar (tel 08432 186 186 from the UK; www.eurostar.com) takes you from London into the heart of Paris to the Gare du Nord in about 2 hours 15 minutes. From here there are good Métro and RER connections, or you can take a taxi. Be sure to beware of touts in the Métro at Gare du Nord trying to sell tickets—there is no guarantee that you will be buying a valid ticket. Use the ticket machines instead.

BUDGET OPTIONS

Within Europe, low-cost airlines such as easyJet (www.easyjet.com) and Ryanair (www.ryanair.com) offer some highly attractive and competitive prices that can sometimes beat the cost of travelling by train. But the tickets are not always bargains; they are priced according to availability and demand. As always, it is usually best to book as far in advance as possible. Keep in mind that Ryanair flies in and out of Beauvais airport, 70km (43 miles) from Paris, so the low cost of a ticket may not be worth the time lost in travelling back and forth to the airport. EasyJet uses Roissy Charles de Gaulle airport.

VISA AND TRAVEL INSURANCE

Visas are not required for EU, US or Canadian nationals, but you will need a valid passport. (Always check the latest requirements before you travel.) EU citizens receive reduced-cost medical treatment with the European Health Insurance Card (EHIC). Full insurance is still strongly advised and is essential for all other travellers.

Getting Around

- Office du Tourisme de Paris ✉ 25 rue des Pyramides, 75001 ☎ No phone; www.parisinfo.com 🕐 Jun–Oct daily 9–7; Nov–May daily 10–7 (Sun from 11) 🚇 Pyramides ❓ There are English-speaking staff in the office

VISITORS WITH DISABILITIES

Paris has a mixed record on access and amenities. On the Métro, only the Meteor line (No. 14) has easy access for people with disabilities. Since 2009 all 63 bus lines in the city are wheelchair accessible and 80 per cent of the bus stops have been adapted to suit. RATP's Les Compagnons du Voyage (☎ 01 58 76 08 33; www.compagnons.com) provides companions for visitors with disabilities (if not in an electric wheelchair), but for a fee. Two taxi companies, G7 (www.taxis-g7.fr) and Taxis PMR (☎ 06 14 67 75 02); will take wheelchairs.
The website of the Paris Tourist Office (www.parisinfo.com) has useful information for visitors with disabilities, including a list of accessible sights.

MÉTRO

The best way to travel around Paris is by Métro or RER, two separate but linked systems (www.ratp.fr). The RER is the suburban line, which passes through the heart of the city. The Métro is the underground system, with 14 main lines and 303 stations. Both are inexpensive and efficient, and free maps of all the routes are available at station ticket windows. Any place is within easy walking distance of a Métro or RER station. Both systems function the same way and the tickets are interchangeable within the city. It is cheaper to buy a *carnet* of 10 tickets than to buy each ticket separately.

- Métro lines are always identified by their destination and a number; connections are shown in *correspondances* panels displayed on the platform.
- Blue *sortie* signs show the exits.
- The first Métros run at 5.30am, and the last around 1.15am (2.15am Fri and Sat).
- Keep your ticket until you exit—it has to be re-slotted on the RER, and ticket inspectors prowl the Métro.
- Try to avoid rush hours: 8–9.30am and 4.30–7pm.

TICKETS AND PASSES

- Tickets and passes function for Métro, buses, trams and RER.
- One ticket (€1.70) gives access to zones 1 and 2 of the Métro network, the RER within Paris, trams, Parisian and suburban buses. A *carnet* of 10 tickets is €12.70.
- Single tickets (known as Ticket t+) are only valid for a single journey without changing between bus, Métro, tram and RER.
- Prices of passes and suburban RER tickets depend on how many travel zones you intend to pass through.
- Mobilis is a one-day pass, valid on Métro, buses and RER.
- A Paris Visite card gives unlimited travel for one, two, three or five days plus discounts at certain monuments, but you need to do a lot of travelling to make it pay.

● *Navigo Découverte* travel cards for visitors are obtainable from stations and valid for a week *(Forfait Navigo Semaine)* or month *(Forfait Navigo Mois)* and vary in price according to the zones you select. You'll need a passport photo and the card itself costs €5.

BATOBUS

Travelling by Batobus—a river shuttle boat—is fun (Apr–Aug daily 10–9.30, every 20 minutes; Sep–Mar daily 10–7, every 25 minutes). It stops at the Eiffel Tower, Musée d'Orsay, Saint-Germain-des-Prés, Notre-Dame, Jardin des Plantes, Hôtel de Ville, Louvre and Champs-Élysées. You can join at any point. An all-day ticket costs €15 (tel 0825 01 01 01; www.batobus.com).

BICYCLES

Bicycles are available at self-service stations across Paris as part of the Vélib' hire scheme (www.velib.paris.fr). There's a hire station every 300m (330 yards) where you can select a one-day (€1.70) or seven-day (€8) ticket; major cards are accepted. Thereafter the first half-hour of each ride is free.

TAXIS

Taxis can be hailed in the street if the roof sign is illuminated or can be found at most main attractions in taxi ranks. There are three different tariffs in central Paris: A applies Mon–Sat 10am–5pm; B applies Mon–Sat 5pm–10pm, Sun 7am–midnight and 24 hours on public holidays Mon–Sat; C applies Sun midnight–7am. There are extra charges for the 4th and 5th passengers, and for luggage over 5kg. Taxi drivers expect tips of 10 per cent.
● The initial fee for hiring a taxi is €2.40 and the minimum fare is €6.40. Tariff A is €0.96 per km, B €1.21 and C €1.47. If luggage is more than 5kg there is an excess of €1.
● Taxi ranks that have telephones can be called on 01 45 30 30 30. Select your *arrondissement* with the help of the voice server, who will then put you through to the closest rank.

● An International Student Identity Card can reduce cinema charges, entrance to museums and air and rail travel.
● MIJE (Maison Internationale de la Jeunesse et des Étudiants) ✉ 13 blvd Beaumarchais, 75004 ☎ 01 42 74 23 45; www.mije.com 🚇 Bastille ⏰ Daily 7am–1am. Three hostels for young people in the heart of Paris.
● CIDJ (Centre d'Information et de Documentation Jeunesse) ✉ 101 quai Branly, 75015 ☎ 01 44 49 12 00; www.cidj.com 🚇 Bir-Hakeim ⏰ Mon–Wed, Fri 10–6, Thu 1–6, Sat 9.30–1). Youth information office for jobs, courses, sport.

Essential Facts

MONEY

The euro is the official currency of France. There are bank notes in denominations of 5, 10, 20, 50, 100, 200 and 500 euros and coins in denominations of 1, 2, 5, 10, 20 and 50 cents and 1 and 2 euros.

TIPPING

In every restaurant, by law, a 15 per cent service charge and all relevant taxes are already in the prices on the menu. If the service was especially pleasant, or if you feel odd about leaving nothing, then you can leave another couple of euros or 5 per cent. In taxis it is customary to give the driver a 10 per cent tip, but only if you are happy with the service.

CREDIT CARDS
● Credit cards are widely accepted.
● VISA cards are the most widely accepted and can be used in cash dispensers. Make sure you know your international PIN. MasterCard and Diners Club are also widely accepted.
● American Express is less common, so Amex cardholders needing cash should use Bureau de Change Kanoo, 11 rue Scribe, 75009; tel 0153 30 99 00; Métro Opéra.

ETIQUETTE
● Shake hands on introduction and on leaving; once you know people well replace this with a peck on both cheeks.
● Always use *vous* unless the other person breaks into *tu*.
● It is polite to add *Monsieur, Madame* or *Mademoiselle* when addressing strangers.
● Always say *bonjour* and *au revoir* in shops.
● When calling waiters, use *Monsieur* or *Madame* (not *garçon*).
● Dress carefully. More emphasis is put on grooming in France than in other countries.

FOREIGN EXCHANGE
● Only banks with Change signs change foreign currency/traveller's cheques; a passport is necessary. Bureaux de change are open longer hours but rates can be poorer. Rates for cashing euro traveller's cheques can be high.
● Airport and station exchange desks are open daily 6 or 6.30am to 10 or 10.30pm.

MEDICINES AND MEDICAL TREATMENT
● Minor ailments can often be treated at pharmacies.
● Public hospitals have a 24-hour emergency service *(urgences)* and specialist doctors. Payment is made on the spot, but if you are hospitalized see the *assistante sociale* to arrange payment through your insurance.
● House calls are made by SOS Médecins, tel 01 47 07 77 77 or 0820 33 24 24; for dental problems SOS Dentaire; tel 01 43 37 51 00.

• 24-hour pharmacy: Les Champs Dhéry, 84 avenue des Champs-Élysées, 75008; tel 01 45 62 02 41.

• Publicis drugstore, 133 avenue des Champs-Élysées (tel 01 44 43 79 00) is a pharmacy, café, newsagent and tobacconist, open until 2am.

• Pharmacies display a green cross outside.

NATIONAL HOLIDAYS

• 1 January, Easter Monday, 1 May, 8 May, Ascension (a Thursday in May), Whit Monday (late May or early June), 14 July, 15 August, 1 November, 11 November, 25 December.

• Sunday services for public transport operate; many local shops, restaurants and even large stores disregard national holidays.

POST OFFICES

• Stamps can be bought at *tabacs*; post mail in any yellow mailbox.

• All post offices offer express courier post (Chronopost), and photocopy machines.

EMERGENCY NUMBERS

• Crisis-line in English: SOS Help ☎ 01 46 21 46 46 🕐 3pm–11pm
• Police ☎ 17
• Any emergency ☎ 112
• Ambulance (SAMU) ☎ 15
• Fire (*sapeurs pompiers*) ☎ 18
• Anti-poison ☎ 01 40 05 48 48
• Police lost-property office is ✉ 36 rue des Morillons, 75015 ☎ 08 21 00 25 25

ELECTRICITY

• Voltage is 220V; French sockets take plugs with two round pins.

PLACES OF WORSHIP

Protestant churches	American Church ✉ 65 quai d'Orsay, 75007 ☎ 01 40 62 05 04 🚇 Invalides
	Saint George's English Church ✉ 7 rue Auguste Vacquerie, 75016 ☎ 01 47 20 22 51 🚇 Charles de Gaulle–Étoile, Kléber
	The Scots Kirk ✉ 17 rue Bayard, 75008 ☎ 01 48 78 47 94 🚇 Franklin D. Roosevelt, Champs-Élysées–Clemenceau
Jewish	Synagogue ✉ 10 rue Pavée, 75004 ☎ No phone 🚇 St-Paul
Muslim	Grande Mosquée de Paris ✉ 2 bis place du Puits-de-l'Ermite, 75005 ☎ 01 45 35 97 33 🚇 Place Monge

For Catholic churches, see the individual entries in the Paris by Area section of this book. The Tourist Office has details of other places of worship.

EMBASSIES/CONSULATES

British Embassy	✉ 35 rue du Faubourg Saint-Honoré, 75008 ☎ 01 44 51 31 00
British Consulate	✉ 16 rue d'Anjou, 75008 ☎ 01 44 51 31 00
US Embassy	✉ 2 avenue Gabriel, 75008 ☎ 01 43 12 22 22
US Consulate	✉ 4 avenue Gabriel, 75008 ☎ 01 43 12 22 22
Canadian Embassy	✉ 35 avenue Montaigne, 75008 ☎ 01 44 43 29 00
Australian Embassy	✉ 4 rue Jean-Rey, 75015 ☎ 01 40 59 33 00
New Zealand Embassy	✉ 7ter rue Léonard-de-Vinci, 75016 ☎ 01 45 01 43 43

OPENING HOURS

● Banks: Mon–Fri 9–12.30, 2–5. Closed on public holidays and often the preceding afternoon.
● Post offices: Mon–Fri 8–7, Sat 8–12. The main post office (✉ 52 rue du Louvre, 75001) provides an overnight service (they close briefly 6am–7.30am) for post, telegrams and telephone.
● Shops: Mon–Sat 9–7 or 10–8. Some close Mon and an hour at lunch.
● Museums: national museums close on Tue, municipal museums on Mon. Individual opening hours vary.

PRESS

● Main dailies are *Le Monde* (serious, centrist), *Libération* (left-wing) and *Le Figaro* (right-wing).
● For weekly listings of cultural events, buy a copy of *Pariscope* (the most popular listings magazine) or *L'Officiel des Spectacles*.
● Central newspaper kiosks and newsagents stock European dailies (widely available on the day of issue) and *USA Today*.
● Visit www.trouverlapresse.com to find out exactly where you can buy your favourite publication.

PUBLIC TOILETS

● Public toilet booths are free and are generally well maintained, although they are not particularly plentiful.
● Every café has a toilet (ask for *'Les toilettes, s'il vous plaît?'*), but order a drink first.

SENSIBLE PRECAUTIONS

● Watch wallets and handbags as pickpockets are active, particularly in busy bars, flea markets, cinemas, the Métro, rail stations and the airport.
● Keep traveller's-cheque numbers separate from the cheques.
● It is important to make a declaration at a local *commissariat* (police station) to claim losses on your insurance.
● Women are generally safe travelling alone or together, although the same risks apply as in any city in western Europe. Deal with any unwanted attention firmly and politely. Avoid the Métro late at night, although it's often busy.

TELEPHONES

● Most phone booths use Orange cards (*télécarte* for 50 or 120 units), sold at post offices, *tabacs* or main Métro stations.
● To call France from the UK dial 00 33—omit the first zero from the number. To call the UK from France, dial 00 44—omit the first zero.
● To call France from the US dial 011 33, then leave out the first zero. To call the US from France dial 00 1 followed by the number.
● All numbers in the Île-de-France, including Paris, start with 01 unless at extra rates, when they start with 08; some are toll-free.
● Numbers in the French provinces begin with: 02 Northwest, 03 Northeast, 04 Southeast, 05 Southwest.

TICKETS

● The Paris Museum Pass (www.parismuseumpass.fr) gives access to 60 museums. It is valid for 2, 4 or 6 days. You can buy it online or at tourist offices, museums and Fnac shops.

Words and Phrases

BASIC VOCABULARY

oui/non	*yes/no*
s'il vous plaît	*please*
merci	*thank you*
excusez-moi	*excuse me*
pardon	*I'm sorry*
bonjour	*hello, good morning*
bonsoir	*good evening*
au revoir	*good-bye*
de rien/avec plaisir	*you're welcome*
parlez-vous anglais?	*do you speak English?*
je ne comprends pas	*I don't understand*
combien?	*how much?*
trop cher	*too expensive*
je voudrais...	*I'd like...*
où est/sont...?	*where is/are ...?*
ici/là	*here/there*
tournez à gauche/droite	*turn left/right*
tout droit	*straight on*
quand?	*when?*
aujourd'hui	*today*
hier	*yesterday*
demain	*tomorrow*
combien de temps?	*how long?*
à quelle heure?	*at what time?*
à quelle heure	*what time do you*
ouvrez/fermez- vous?	*open/close?*
avez-vous...?	*do you have ...?*
une chambre simple	*a single room*
une chambre double	*a double room*
avec/sans salle de	*with/without*
bains	*bathroom*
le petit déjeuner	*breakfast*
le déjeuner	*lunch*
le dîner	*dinner*
c'est combien?	*how much is this?*
puis-je réserver une table	*I'd like to book a table*
une bouteille/un verre de...	*a bottle/glass of...*
acceptez-vous des	*do you take credit*
cartes de crédit?	*cards?*
j'ai besoin d'un	*I need a*
médecin/dentiste	*doctor/dentist*
pouvez-vous m'aider?	*can you help me?*
où est l'hôpital?	*where is the hospital?*
où est le commissariat?	*where is the police*
	station?

NUMBERS

un	1
deux	2
trois	3
quatre	4
cinq	5
six	6
sept	7
huit	8
neuf	9
dix	10
onze	11
douze	12
treize	13
quatorze	14
quinze	15
seize	16
dix-sept	17
dix-huit	18
dix-neuf	19
vingt	20
vingt-et-un	21
trente	30
quarante	40
cinquante	50
soixante	60
soixante-dix	70
quatre-vingts	80
quatre-vingt-dix	90
cent	100
mille	1,000

MONTHS

janvier	January
février	February
mars	March
avril	April
mai	May
juin	June
juillet	July
août	August
septembre	September
octobre	October
novembre	November
décembre	December

Index

The Automobile Association would like to thank the following photographers, companies and picture libraries for their assistance in the preparation of this book.

2i Paris Tourist Office/Marc Bertrand; **2ii** AA/K Blackwell; **2iii** AA/K Blackwell; **2iv** Hemis/Alamy; **2v** AA/ M Jourdan; **3i** AA/K Blackwell; **3ii** AA/K Blackwell; **3iii** AA/K Blackwell; **3iv** AA/K Blackwell; **4** AA/K Blackwell; **5** Paris Tourist Office/Marc Bertrand; **6/7t** AA/K Blackwell; **6/7ct** PARAMOUNT/THE KOBAL COLLECTION; **6/7cb** THE KOBAL COLLECTION; **6/7b** Kristjan Porm/Alamy; **7ct** AA/K Blackwell; **7cb** MGM/THE KOBAL COLLECTION; **8/9t** AA/K Blackwell; **8c** AA/K Blackwell; **8/9b** AA/K Paterson; **9ct** AA/K Blackwell; **9cb** AA/M Jourdan; **10l** AA/K Blackwell; **10r** The Bridgeman Art Library; **11** Keystone/Getty Images; **12** AA/K Blackwell; **14** AA/K Blackwell; **15tl** AA/K Blackwell; **15cl** AA/K Blackwell; **15tr** AA/K Blackwell; **15cr** AA/K Blackwell; **16l** Centre Pompidou; **16tr** AA/T Souter; **16/17** Susana Vázquez; **17l** AA/C Sawyer; **17tr** Susana Vázquez; **17cr** Centre Pompidou; **18t** AA/K Blackwell; **18b** AA/K Blackwell; **19tl** AA/K Blackwell; **19cl** AA/K Blackwell; **19r** AA/K Blackwell; **20l** AA/K Blackwell; **20/21t** AA/K Blackwell; **20c** AA/K Blackwell; **21c** AA/K Blackwell; **21r** AA/M Jourdan; **22l** AA/M Jourdan; **22tr** AA; **22cr** AA/K Blackwell; **23tl** AA/K Blackwell; **23cl** AA/K Blackwell; **23r** AA/K Blackwell; **24/25** age fotostock/Alamy; **25tr** AA/C Sawyer; **25cr** AA/K Blackwell; **26l** AA/K Blackwell; **26/27t** AA/K Blackwell; **26/27c** AA/K Blackwell; **27t** AA/K Blackwell; **27c** AA/K Blackwell; **28** AA/K Blackwell; **29t** AA/M Jourdan; **29c** AA/K Blackwell; **29r** AA/J Tims; **30l** AA/M Jourdan; **30/31t** AA/M Jourdan; **30/31c** AA/J Tims; **31t** The Bridgeman Art Library; **31c** Susana Vázquez; **32** AA/J Tims; **33tl** AA/K Blackwell; **33t** AA/K Blackwell; **33c** AA/K Blackwell; **34** AA/C Sawyer; **34/35t** AA/K Paterson; **34/35c** AA/M Jourdan; **35t** AA/M Jourdan; **35c** AA/K Paterson; **36** AA/K Blackwell; **36/37** AA/K Blackwell; **37l** AA/K Blackwell; **37tr** AA/K Blackwell; **37cr** AA/K Blackwell; **38l** AA/M Jourdan; **38/9t** Danita Delimont/Alamy; **38/9b** Paris Le Marais/Alamy; **39r** AA/P Kenward; **40** AA/K Blackwell; **41tl** Giraudon/The Bridgeman Art Library ; **41cl** The Art Archive/Alamy; **41r** Hemis/Alamy; **42** AA/K Blackwell; **42/43t** AA/M Jourdan; **42/43c** AA/K Blackwell; **43t** AA/B Rieger; **43cl** AA/K Blackwell; **43cr** AA/K Blackwell; **44** AA/K Blackwell; **45tl** AA/K Blackwell; **45cl** AA/K Blackwell; **45c** Dorothy Alexander/Alamy; **45r** AA/K Blackwell; **46/47** AA/K Blackwell; **47l** AA/K Blackwell; **47r** AA/M Jourdan; **48** AA/T Souter; **48/49t** AA/K Blackwell; **48/49c** AA/M Jourdan; **49** AA/K Blackwell; **50l** AA/K Blackwell; **50r** AA/K Blackwell; **50/51** AA/K Blackwell; **51l** AA/K Blackwell; **51t** AA/M Jourdan; **51c** AA/K Blackwell; **52** AA/C Sawyer; **53l** AA/P Kenward; **53t** Paris Tourist Office/Marc Bertrand; **53c** Andrew Duke/Alamy; **54l** AA/K Blackwell; **54r** Glenn Harper/Alamy; **54/55** Jon Arnold Images Ltd/Alamy; **55** JOHN KELLERMAN/Alamy; **56** AA/K Blackwell; **56/57t** AA/K Blackwell; **56c** AA/K Blackwell; **57l** AA/K Blackwell; **57tr** AA/J Tims; **57cr** AA/J Tims; **58** AA/T Souter; **58/59** AA/K Blackwell; **59tl** AA/K Blackwell; **59tr** AA/K Blackwell; **59cr** AA/K Blackwell; **60** AA/K Blackwell; **60/61t** AA/K Blackwell; **60/61c** AA/K Blackwell; **61t** AA/K Blackwell; **61c** AA/K Blackwell; **62** AA/K Blackwell; **63tl** AA/K Blackwell; **63c** AA/M Jourdan; **63tc** AA/K Blackwell; **63tr** Hemis/Alamy; **64** AA/K Blackwell; **66l** JOHN KELLERMAN/Alamy; **66r** AA/K Blackwell; **67l** AA/K Blackwell; **67r** AA/K Blackwell; **68** AA/K Blackwell; **69l** AA/C Sawyer; **69r** AA/K Blackwell; **70l** AA/K Blackwell; **70r** AA/K Blackwell; **71l** JOHN KELLERMAN/Alamy; **71r** AA/K Blackwell; **72** AA/K Blackwell; **73l** AA/C Sawyer; **73r** AA/M Jourdan; **74l** AA/M Jourdan; **74r** AA/T Souter; **75l** AA/C Sawyer; **75r** AA/K Blackwell; **76** AA/K Blackwell; **77l** AA/D Noble; **77r** AA/D Noble; **78l** Disney Enterprises, Inc.; **78r** Disney Enterprises, Inc.; **79** AA/D Noble; **80** Hemis/Alamy; **82t** AA/K Blackwell; **82b** AA/J Tims; **83t** AA/K Blackwell; **83b** AA/K Blackwell; **86i** AA/K Blackwell; **86ii** AA/K Blackwell; **86iii** AA/M Jourdan; **86iv** AA/K Blackwell; **87** AA/M Jourdan; **88t** Christophe Testi/Alamy; **88b** AA/K Blackwell; **89t** AA/K Blackwell; **89b** AA/C Sawyer; **92i** AA/K Blackwell; **92ii** AA/K Blackwell; **92iii** AA/K Paterson; **92iv** AA/K Blackwell; **92v** AA/K Blackwell; **92vi** AA/K Blackwell; **94t** AA/M Jourdan; **94b** AA/M Jourdan; **95** AA/K Blackwell; **98i** Centre Pompidou; **98ii** AA/M Jourdan; **98iii** AA/K Blackwell; **98iv** Paris Tourist Office/Amélie Dupont ; **100** AA/K Blackwell; **101t** AA/K Blackwell; **101b** AA/K Blackwell; **104i** AA/K Blackwell; **104ii** AA/K Blackwell; **104iii** AA/K Blackwell; **104iv** AA/J Tims; **104v** AA/K Blackwell; **104vi** AA/M Jourdan; **106t** AA/P Enticknap; **106b** AA/M Jourdan; **107t** AA/J Tims; **107b** AA/P Enticknap; **110t** AA/T Souter; **110b** AA/J Tims; **111l** AA/K Blackwell; **111r** AA/C Sawyer; **112t** AA/M Jourdan; **112c** AA/K Blackwell; **112b** AA/M Jourdan; **113t** AA/K Blackwell; **113c** AA/M Jourdan; **116i** AA/K Blackwell; **116ii** AA/K Blackwell; **116iii** AA/K Blackwell; **116iv** AA/K Blackwell; **117** AA/K Blackwell; **118** AA/M Jourdan; **120/121t** Paris Tourist Office/Marc Bertrand; **120/121ct** Paris Tourist Office/David Lefranc; **121ct** AA/C Sawyer; **120cb** AA/C Sawyer; **120/121cb** AA/C Sawyer; **120/121b** AA/C Sawyer; **125** AA/C Sawyer; **127** AA/K Blackwell; **128** AA/K Blackwell; **130** AA/K Blackwell; **132/133t** Paris Tourist Office/David Lefranc; **132ct** Paris Tourist Office/David Lefranc; **132/133ct** AA/K Blackwell; **132/133cb** Paris Tourist Office/Amélie Dupont ; **133cb** AA/P Enticknap; **132b** AA/K Paterson; **133b** AA/K Blackwell; **140** AA/K Blackwell; **142i** AA/K Blackwell; **142ii** AA/K Blackwell; **142iii** AA/K Blackwell; **142iv** AA/K Blackwell; **144** AA/K Blackwell; **147** AA/K Blackwell; **148** AA/K Blackwell; **150** AA/C Sawyer; **152** AA/K Blackwell; **154i** AA/K Blackwell; **154ii** AA/K Blackwell; **154iii** AA/K Blackwell; **154iv** AA/K Blackwell; **160** AA/K Blackwell.

Every effort has been made to trace the copyright holders, and we apologise in advance for any unintentional omissions or errors. We would be pleased to apply any corrections in a following edition of this publication.

Paris 25 Best

WRITTEN BY Fiona Dunlop
ADDITIONAL WRITING BY Neville Walker
UPDATED BY Mike Gerrard
SERIES EDITOR Clare Ashton
COVER DESIGN Chie Ushio, Yuko Inagaki
DESIGN WORK Tracey Butler
IMAGE RETOUCHING AND REPRO Ian Little

Published in the United Kingdom by AA Publishing

ISBN 978-0-8041-4329-5

ELEVENTH EDITION

SPECIAL SALES
This book is available for special discounts for bulk purchases for sales promotions or premiums. For more information, email specialmarkets@randomhouse.com.

Color separation by AA Digital Department
Printed and bound by Leo Paper Products, China

10 9 8 7 6 5 4 3 2 1

A05132
Maps in this title produced from map data © Tele Atlas N.V. 2013   Tele Atlas
Transport map © Communicarta Ltd, UK

Titles in the Series